ry

A Crowdfunder's Strategy Guide

A CROWDFUNDER'S
STRATEGY
GUIDE

BUILD A BETTER BUSINESS
BY BUILDING COMMUNITY

JAMEY STEGMAIER

BK

Berrett–Koehler Publishers, Inc.
a BK Business book

BERRETT-KOEHLER PUBLISHERS, INC.
1333 Broadway, Suite 1000, Oakland, CA 94612-1921
Tel: (510) 817-2277   Fax: (510) 817-2278   www.bkconnection.com

ORDERING INFORMATION
QUANTITY SALES. Special discounts are available on quantity purchases by corporations, associations, and others. For details, contact the "Special Sales Department" at the Berrett-Koehler address above.

INDIVIDUAL SALES. Berrett-Koehler publications are available through most bookstores. They can also be ordered directly from Berrett-Koehler: Tel: (800) 929-2929; Fax: (802) 864-7626; www.bkconnection.com

ORDERS FOR COLLEGE TEXTBOOK/COURSE ADOPTION USE. Please contact Berrett-Koehler: Tel: (800) 929-2929; Fax: (802) 864-7626.

Orders by U.S. trade bookstores and wholesalers. Please contact Ingram Publisher Services, Tel: (800) 509-4887; Fax: (800) 838-1149; E-mail: customer.service@ingrampublisherservices .com; or visit www.ingrampublisherservices.com/Ordering for details about electronic ordering.

Berrett-Koehler and the BK logo are registered trademarks of Berrett-Koehler Publishers, Inc.

Printed in the United States of America

Berrett-Koehler books are printed on long-lasting acid-free paper. When it is available, we choose paper that has been manufactured by environmentally responsible processes. These may include using trees grown in sustainable forests, incorporating recycled paper, minimizing chlorine in bleaching, or recycling the energy produced at the paper mill.

LIBRARY OF CONGRESS CATALOGING-IN-PUBLICATION DATA
Stegmaier, Jamey.
A crowdfunder's strategy guide : build a better business by building community / by Jamey Stegmaier. — First Edition.
      pages cm
Includes bibliographical references and index.
ISBN 978-1-62656-408-4 (pbk. : alk. paper)
1. New business enterprises. 2. New business enterprises—Management. I. Title.
HD62.5.S7413 2015
658.15'224—dc23

2015012407

FIRST EDITION
20 19 18 17 16 15   10 9 8 7 6 5 4 3 2 1

Interior design and production: VJB/Scribe. Copyeditor: John Pierce.
Proofreader: Nancy Bell. Index: George Draffan.
Cover/jacket design: Wes Youssi/M.80 Design.
Author photo: Eric Desmarais.

To all of my fellow creators who put their backers first.

CONTENTS

PREFACE

This book was supposed to be a young adult dystopian novel set in the year 2094.

In March 2012, I was six months into the design and development of Viticulture, the game that would later become the cornerstone of my company, Stonemaier Games. I was burning out. The game was in a pretty good place, but it wasn't ready for Kickstarter, and I had neglected my other creative passion, writing, for a long time.

I had also started to understand how big a commitment it is to design and publish a game, and I was worried that once I went down that path, it would be really difficult to accomplish my lifelong goal of writing a novel.

I'd tried to write novels before. Two of them, specifically. I approached both as epic projects that would take years to complete. I got about halfway through both before I gave up. Other things took priority.

However, I have writer friends who write multiple novels a year. Writer friends with kids. And jobs. And other passions.

So in March 2012, I gave myself two months to write a novel from start to finish. It was my sole focus during that time, other than my day job, eating, and sleeping.

The strategy actually worked! Two months after I started, I put the finishing touches on *Wrinkle*, a novel in which overpopulation results in a significant number of people electively traveling to the future.

As you can see by this book's cover, you're not reading *Wrinkle*. But this book wouldn't exist without *Wrinkle* for several reasons: First, completing a novel after thirty-one years of not completing a novel felt like a full-body cleanse. (That's an assumption—I've never tried a full-body cleanse, unless you count Taco Bell.) I felt unburdened by that long-overdue personal goal, and I was free to go all-in on my Kickstarter campaign for Viticulture. Without a successful campaign for Viticulture, it's likely that none of this—the games, the company, the blog, this book—would exist.

Second, completing *Wrinkle* helped me realize that I was the only person or entity holding myself back from the joy of creating something new. That is the difference between an imaginative person and a creative person—a creative person actually *creates* things. Crossing that threshold prepared me for the creative process that goes hand in hand with being a crowdfunder.

Third, after writing and revising *Wrinkle* in the summer of 2012, the novel came up in conversation with a literary agent I knew through some contacts in the publishing world. Jennifer Chen Tran read the manuscript, gave me some good feedback, and encouraged me to keep working on it.

I stayed in touch with Jennifer over the next year, during which time I ran two successful Kickstarter campaigns and built a strong audience on my blog about crowdfunding.[1] One day, she e-mailed me and asked, "Have you ever thought about writing a book about crowdfunding?"

I had entertained the idea but hadn't seriously considered it. In terms of total content, I had already written a book—all of my blog entries up to that point could fill a large tome.

Jennifer pointed out that the blog is pretty technical—it is mostly a step-by-step guide on how to create a successful crowdfunding project. It doesn't read as a cohesive whole. It doesn't tell a story.

More important, she added, my blog reaches only those who happen to stumble on it. It's a limited audience, mostly tabletop game creators. "Think of the other people you could help by telling your story—and the stories of innovative crowdfunders—in a book," Jennifer said. (I'm paraphrasing here—in reality, about twenty e-mail messages were needed before I fully grasped the concept.)

She was right. The whole goal of the blog was to help other creators, and I was reaching only a very small subset at that point. So I started writing this book for all types of entrepreneurs who are intrigued by the idea of crowdfunding, particularly those who are open to the idea that creating something is less about *them*—the creators—and more about *others*—the backers, customers, fans, and supporters who share a passion for the thing the creators are trying to make.

If you like this book, you can thank Jennifer Chen Tran and my readers for inspiring and encouraging me to create something for you. If you don't like it, you can blame its existence on the popularity of the YA dystopian genre.

INTRODUCTION

I've run seven successful Kickstarter projects that together have raised more than a million dollars, and I've consulted on and backed countless others. The success of those campaigns has allowed me to run my board game publishing company, Stonemaier Games, full-time.

Throughout this book I refer to Stonemaier Games in terms of "we" and "our," since I'm not alone in this endeavor. I have a business partner (Alan Stone), an advisory board, hundreds of "ambassadors," and thousands of backers (crowdfunding customers).

I designed three of our games—Viticulture, Euphoria, and Tuscany—as well as a game accessory, the Treasure Chest, all four of which have a total of nearly fifty thousand copies in print. To put it in perspective, that's really good for a small publishing company that has been around for about two years and really bad for, say, Hasbro.

I write a crowdfunding blog where I share my insights, mistakes, research, and observations to provide a detailed template for how other crowdfunders might, I hope, achieve success. When I refer to "the blog" in this book, I'm talking about the Kickstarter Lessons website, not my personal blog.[1] That blog is mostly about my cats.

The crowdfunding blog serves as a complement to this book, but the two are very different. The blog is a step-by-step guide to creating a crowdfunding project and running a campaign. I've been told that it contains an almost overwhelming amount of information. So for the readers of this book, I've condensed those 125 lessons down to 125 sentences (well, I *tried* to limit myself to one sentence per lesson), found in the Resources section of this book.

1

They're not a replacement for the full entries, nor do they explain the logic behind the lessons, but if you trust me by the time you reach the end of this book, they're there for you to consider.

A Crowdfunder's Strategy Guide is much more anecdotal than my blog. Whenever I read a book like this, I find myself skipping over the pedantic parts to get to the concrete, real-life examples. So I've tried to fill the book with stories, not lessons.

Several projects I feature in this book fall into the category of "megaprojects." These are projects that wildly overfunded. You can learn a lot from these projects, but it's important to remember that correlation does not equal causation, especially when comparing your project with these. Just because megaproject A launched on, say, July 8 and raised $10 million does not mean that if you also launch your project on July 8, you will raise $10 million, too.

When you research megaprojects, dig under the surface a bit before drawing any conclusions. Read the project updates, poke around for a postmortem or lessons-learned post, look into past or future projects to see how their creators' methods changed over time, and so on. Megaprojects are often successful *despite* their flaws and deviations from best practices, and it's up to you to distinguish how they deviated and the resulting impact.

The one common thread between the blog and this book is my belief that you will significantly increase your odds of crowdfunding success if you focus on building community, empathizing with supporters, and developing trust-based relationships. Whenever you're faced with a decision—big or small—simply ask yourself, "What's the right thing for my backers?"

I will systematically prove to you in every chapter of this book that by putting your backers first and connecting with individual backers, you will be a better, happier, more successful creator.

Even though the stories and lessons in this book will increase your odds of crowdfunding success, nothing is guaranteed. This is actually the great thing about crowdfunding: the crowd will vote with their dollars to tell you whether there is demand for whatever it is you're trying to create. If you put in the legwork and present your idea well, but it still doesn't successfully fund, that's a sign that the world isn't interested. And that's okay. It's a lot better to determine what the demand is before you invest thousands of dollars to make something.

Last, it's important to note that a lot of the examples in this book are tabletop game projects. I run tabletop game projects and own a board game company, so it makes sense that I pay more attention to that category and hobnob with other tabletop game creators more than others. However, the vast majority of the examples I use can apply to *any* category, and I've made sure to include plenty of stories from other categories, not just to reach various types of creators, but also because these stories fascinate me. I've learned just as much from campaigns unrelated to games as I have from those that are.

Now, my friends, it's time to make this book all about *you*.

CHAPTER 1

You Don't Need to Launch Today

**The second-most successful Kickstarter project of all time origi-
nally launched six months too soon and failed.** But when the Coolest cooler relaunched half a year later, it raised $13,285,226 from
62,642 backers.

One of the biggest mistakes people make when launching a
crowdfunding project is to launch too soon. While the Coolest
cooler is an outlier, given its epic level of success, it serves as a great
example of how *not* launching today can make a huge impact on
your dream project.

FIGURE 1. The Coolest cooler, the product behind one of the most successful crowdfunding campaigns ever held. Reproduced courtesy of
Ryan Grepper.

Ryan Grepper is an inventor in Portland, Oregon, who came up with the idea of the Coolest (fig. 1). With his innovative design, which features a built-in blender, a Bluetooth speaker, an LED light under the lid, a phone recharger, and more, he targeted Kickstarter as a way of gauging demand for the product. Ryan calls Kickstarter the "Skymall of the future," where people go to find and influence tomorrow's products today.

Ryan Grepper launched the original Coolest cooler Kickstarter campaign on November 26, 2013. With a goal of $125,000, the project raised a fair amount (just over $102,000) — enough to indicate market demand — but ultimately it didn't fund.

When I spoke with Ryan in October 2014, he was candid about the experience. He confirmed that seasonality had a huge affect on the popularity of the summer campaign for the Coolest cooler. His original strategy was to schedule the crowdfunding campaign so that the product could be manufactured and delivered in time for the relevant season, but he realized that people aren't really thinking about keeping things cool when they're shoveling snow off their driveways.

After the unsuccessful campaign, Ryan got to work. He improved the design of the cooler and refined the project page, all while continuing to engage the original backers. Before relaunching the campaign in the summer, he used a service called PressFriendly to connect with bloggers and journalists who had written about innovative summertime products in the past. He identified a few key media targets and, as a nod to the cooler's built-in blender, sent each of them a package containing margarita mix, a small bottle of Jose Cuervo, and a bag of water, with a note saying, "If you had a Coolest cooler, you'd be drinking a margarita right now."

After the unsuccessful funding of the first campaign, Ryan was nervous leading up to the relaunch. His concerns were quickly assuaged, though, as all of his hard work the previous seven months translated into more than $300K on the first day, in early July 2014. In the peak of summer, keeping things cool was a top priority for anyone living in the northern hemisphere. The project rocketed past the million-dollar mark on day 2 and past $2 million on day 3.

Ryan had planned to send personal thank-you messages to each backer, but he soon realized that wasn't feasible. In fact, despite his careful planning, he was deep over his head in replying to the flood of comments and messages he was receiving.

So he took action. It was summer break for college students, so he hired some neighborhood kids to form a customer-service team. He also tapped some international connections to provide 24/7 support to backers while the lights were out in Portland. Working off an FAQ and a shared Gmail account, Ryan and his team worked through the backlog of thousands of messages in a matter of days.

With thousands of backers joining the project every day, gathering feedback and involving backers in product development—standard methods for building community on Kickstarter—were quite a challenge. The top request that Ryan and his team received was to add a solar panel to the top of the cooler, but Ryan determined that doing so wasn't feasible. Instead, his team tried to concentrate all of this creative energy into backer polls, like the one team members ran in the middle of the campaign for new cooler colors. Ryan made sure to let backers know through project updates and videos that he was listening to their input, and several suggestions made during the campaign (hinge strength, handle configuration, phone dock design, etc.) would impact the final model.

The campaign showed no sign of slowing down. It eventually eclipsed the previous top-funding project, the Pebble smartwatch, and the campaign ended with more than $13 million. Pretty impressive for a project that didn't reach its $125,000 funding goal just six months earlier.

When You Control Time, There Is No Such Thing As "Last Minute"

Launching too soon is one of the most common mistakes made by crowdfunders—and perhaps the easiest to avoid. Creators contact me regularly asking for the same advice: "I'm launching my crowd-funding project today, and I just found your blog—do you have any last-minute feedback?"

Yes, I have some last-minute feedback: Don't launch today if you're doing anything "last minute." Simply shift your artificially determined launch date to another day. Easy. Done.

Ninety-nine percent of the time when I get a message like that, I know something is wrong without even looking at the project page. Because if you have the mindset that you're somehow on a deadline for launching your project, you're setting yourself up for failure from the start. Not necessarily catastrophic failure, but you're not doing everything you can to make your project a success.

A growing wealth of resources is out there for the steps you can take to increase the chances that your crowdfunding project will be successful. It's important that you discover them *months* before you launch your campaign. So if today is the day you've discovered a key resource, add two to three months to today, and you'll have your new launch day.

Not convinced? Here's a list of some of the things you need to do before you launch your project. If you have not done these things, do not launch your project today.

The Definitive Prelaunch Checklist

- **Start a blog** focusing on creating content that is interesting and useful to other people and write one to three entries per week for three months.

- **Hunt down and subscribe to at least twenty blogs** related to your project. Read them every day. Comment on at least one a day. Do not think of this as networking. Think of it as reading about a subject you love and interacting with people who share your passion.

- **Read every Kickstarter Lesson on my blog,** listen to a number of Richard Bliss's Funding the Dream podcast episodes, and read James Mathe's blog about Kickstarter.[1]

- **Back ten to twenty crowdfunding projects** and read every update in real time, taking note of when you reach the point at which you have the intense desire to unsubscribe. According to statistics pulled from John Coveyou's extensive Kickstarter data mining,[2] your chance of successfully funding your first project if you've backed only one project is 23 percent. If you've backed between eleven and twenty-five projects, your chance nearly doubles, to 55 percent. This isn't a token correlation—it's an indication that creators who take the time to back other projects and learn from them day by day are significantly better prepared.

- **Add value to something that's important to a stranger every day,** for at least two months. Share a crowdfunding project you love. Be active and positive on a message board or comment section. Send a message to a project creator and tell her what you love about what she's doing. Proofread and offer feedback on another crowdfunder's preview page. Contribute to a conversation on the Kickstarter Best Practices Facebook group. Play-test someone else's game. Do all these things without asking for anything in return or even mentioning that you are working on your own project.

- **Create a spreadsheet of at least ten successful crowdfunding projects** that are similar to your project to compare them with one another.

- **Create an extensive budget for your project,** factoring in a number of different outcomes and what they mean for production and shipping. This step is where you need to figure out how you're going to ship your product around the world in a way that is efficient and cost-effective for you and your backers. Don't wait to do this after your project has funded or launched.

- **Pay a professional artist and designer** to create some really attractive, eye-catching art to show off on your project page. Find an artist you love and pay him. Don't go cheap on art. Make sure that art is actually good by seeking feedback from people who don't care at all about your feelings (i.e., not friends or family).

- **Send out samples of your product to several high-impact bloggers,** podcasters, or YouTube channels. For game creators, this means sending full game prototypes. Don't send the samples out of the blue—send them only to people you've been a fan of for a while and have interacted with in some context.

- **Share your project preview page with at least twenty people,** asking for their feedback. Ask three specific questions and two open-ended questions. If there are consistencies in the answers you get, pay really close attention and do something about it even if you disagree.

- **Send out personalized press releases to fifteen to twenty blogs** and relevant news outlets at least one week before your project launches.

- **Clear your schedule for launch day** so that you can spend all day sending personal invitations to share your dream with your friends and family and respond to individual backers as they pledge.

If you have not done these things, you are significantly decreasing the chance that you'll reach your funding goal. Period. All of the reasons you have for launching today are nowhere near as important to the success of your project as tackling all the steps on this list.

Let's look at some of the reasons people give for sticking with a self-created deadline even when it no longer makes sense:

"I already told everyone it's going to launch today."

The idea behind announcing an upcoming launch day is good—you build anticipation for your project, you release it to the world as announced, and then you hope to have a successful launch day. In essence, that's a good thing.

But the trouble is that you can sometimes forget that you're the one who creates those deadlines in the first place. No one is holding you to them, yet I get that sense from a number of project creators. They've been giving people a certain date for a while, and if they miss that artificial deadline, they feel like it ruins everything.

Let me assure you: nothing bad will happen if you don't launch on the day you said you would.

Plus, crowdfunding sites now allow people to press a button on your preview page and get a notification when you launch your project. So if you've shared your preview page with your friends and fans, they're going to get an e-mail when you're ready to launch.

"I have to launch today or I'll run into a bad time of the month or the year for a crowdfunding project."

Perhaps you've read somewhere that projects make more money or get more backers if they're launched at a certain time of the year—that you should avoid launching in certain months or times of the month. Well, I'm here to tell you that if you have a great project and you've put in the legwork, timing hardly matters at all (with the exception of seasonality, as you saw with the Coolest). There's no magical formula for the month or time of month, so stop focusing on that and focus on making an awesome project.

"I have to launch today because I need the money ASAP."

Your livelihood should not depend on a single crowdfunding campaign. You're raising money to create something, not to fund your personal expenses. Most people will have tough financial times at some point in their lives. Those times suck, but they're neither the time nor the reason to launch a crowdfunding project. Figure out your personal finances and keep them separate from your project when it's ready to launch on its own merit.

"My project isn't 100 percent ready, but I'll fix it during the campaign."

It's a good thing if your *product* isn't 100 percent complete. Leave some wiggle room for feedback from backers and improvement. But the *project* should be 100 percent complete when you launch. Sure, it will evolve over time, but the first few days of a project are important. Don't waste them on a subpar project page.

"I have to launch today or my production schedule is ruined."

I saved this one for last because *I did this*. I wanted to get Euphoria to backers before Christmas, so I had to finish the project on June 12 and send it to my manufacturer by June 22. It was such a tight schedule, and we barely managed to make it for 95 percent of backers.

But here's the deal: No matter how well you've planned your project, you simply do not know what awaits you in production and shipping. There are so many variables. If you really want to target certain dates — say, a release at a big convention — your production schedule should have at least one to two months of buffer room.

I wrote this chapter just in case someone recommended this book to you the week you planned to launch your project. It's going to be okay. You don't need to launch today. You have this book now. You have the gift of time: two to three months extra to prep your project for a successful launch. You have the definitive prelaunch checklist of easy-to-accomplish steps. In this book's Resources section, you have the "One-Week Checklist," a list of things to do in the final week leading up to your project.

After all of that prep work, when you finally press the Launch button, it's going to be spectacular.

CHAPTER 2

The Crowd Is the New Gatekeeper

You don't sleep much the night before you click the Launch button for your career.

That was the situation I found myself in the night of March 11, 2014. I had quit my day job three months before to focus on my fledgling board-game company, Stonemaier Games. I had run three successful Kickstarter campaigns at that point and was selling my games to distributors and retailers, but the longevity of my full-time career as a board-game publisher was largely dependent on the success of the Kickstarter campaign I was set to launch the next day for a game called Tuscany (fig. 2).

At 5:30 that morning I woke up with a start, absolutely convinced that it was 8:30 and I had missed my alarm. Eventually I

FIGURE 2. The box for Tuscany: Expand the World of Viticulture.

coaxed myself back to sleep, woke up on schedule, and sent out an e-mail notification to my e-newsletter subscribers informing them that Tuscany would be live on Kickstarter in a few minutes. If I raised $20,000 over the next twenty-eight days, I would be able to make Tuscany a reality.

Then I clicked the Launch button and held my breath.

I didn't have time to watch the first few pledges come in because I needed to update the Kickstarter widgets and links on my company website and fill in the FAQ on the Kickstarter project page. (You can't do that before you launch.) When I finished these tasks, I checked the project page.

In sixteen minutes, Tuscany had reached the funding goal of $20,000.

Twenty minutes later, the funding total doubled, and it had tripled by the end of the first hour. The comments section on the Kickstarter project page and our Facebook page were abuzz with people talking about how quickly the project funded. At the twenty-four-hour mark, Tuscany had raised more than $158,000 from 1,622 backers, a number that well exceeded my best projections.

I'd like to share with you how I did it. Here's a hint: it's not about the money.

The Birth of Crowdfunding

When I was growing up in Virginia in the 1980s and '90s, I had two creative passions: writing and designing board games. My first book, which I wrote when I was five, was a full-color, limited-edition, custom-bound hardback about a rocket ship taking off and flying into outer space. A few years later I designed my first board game, a Camelot-inspired rip-off of Monopoly called Medieval Quest.

I had a skewed perception of what it meant to be a professional writer or game designer. I thought that I just needed to create one big hit and I'd be set for life.

You know as well as I do that my assumption couldn't have been further from the truth. Even the most popular authors continue to write not only for the money but because they love to write. And very few board-game designers are able to sustain their families from game royalties alone. Writers, designers, and other artists have to work really, really hard to make a consistent living from their art.

That's where crowdfunding platforms have started to reshape the ways creative people can make their passion projects come to life. Anyone can start a crowdfunding project. You set a funding goal and a time frame, create a project page, and list a few rewards that backers receive in return for their support. It's not a charity, and it's not equity investing—it's a platform for funding your dream.

However, dreams aren't free. They take a lot of hard work. This is important to remember when you look at megasuccessful crowdfunding campaigns. You might look at the Pebble campaign[1] (over $10 million raised from 68,929 backers) and think, "If I slap something together on Kickstarter, I can be a millionaire!" I want to debunk that assumption.

Five Unalienable Truths about Crowdfunding

1. **Community building is more important than cash**   If your focus is on people, not on money, you will be significantly more successful—*crowd* precedes *funding* in *crowdfunding*.

2. **It's not easy money**   For a successful project—or a megasuccessful one—you will work harder than you ever have. If you don't have much free time, running a crowdfunding campaign is extremely difficult.

3. **You need a polished, tested concept, not just an idea**   It's great that you have a cool idea, and crowdfunding is the perfect place to gauge demand for a new innovation. But you need to actually design, develop, and prove that you have something worth people's hard-earned funds *before* you launch the campaign.

4 **Making something awesome is expensive**   If you create something that's awesome enough and price it fairly to compel thousands of people to pledge to receive it, the vast majority of the revenue will go toward actually making that awesome thing, not into your pocket.

5. **Crowdfunding is just the beginning**   True crowdfunding success means funding something people continue to want even after the campaign ends. Do you want to make one product or launch an entire business?

Conversely, there are a number of benefits to crowdfunding.

Top Ten Reasons to Crowdfund the Creation of Something New

1. **Build community**   Crowdfunding allows creative people to build a community around their creations. This can lead to much greater success in the long run if you're launching or expanding a business through a crowdfunded project because you have a passionate group of fans supporting you (and holding you accountable).

2. **Gauge demand**   You might have an idea that you think is really cool, but you don't know how the general public will

receive it. There's no better way to find out than asking people to pay for something that doesn't exist yet.

3. **Low financial risk**   If you need to raise a lot of money to create something new, rather than take out a loan or put your own money at risk, crowdfunding provides a way to raise funds without giving up equity in your endeavor. Plus, the whole idea of the "funding goal" helps creators avoid situations where they raise *some* money but not *enough* to fully realize their dream.

4. **Create something better**   Stretch goals—enhancements made to the product after certain funding thresholds have been reached—help you make the best possible version of the product. For example, if prefunding exceeds the amount needed for the minimum print run of a board game, the cost per unit decreases and you can add more and better components to every game.

5. **Business training wheels**   Starting a business is hard, but a crowdfunding campaign gives you the opportunity to learn how to launch a company with the "training wheels" still on. You have a big group of people there to point you in the right direction, and you usually have plenty of time to figure things out. Plus, if your original campaign doesn't fund, you can try again.

6. **Direct access to customers**   Say you create a new product and sell it to Walmart. You know nothing about the people who buy the product. But with crowdfunding, you know tons of information about every single customer. That data is incredibly helpful.

7. **Promotion**   Crowdfunding websites are platforms, not promoters of products. But a lot of people browse those websites

to discover innovative products and share their passions, so you have access to a broad range of customers who wouldn't otherwise hear of you.

8. **Urgency** The limited-time aspect of a crowdfunding campaign creates a level of urgency that preorders cannot replicate.

9. **Trust in the platform** Remember when people were really hesitant to enter their credit card information online? Now we don't think twice about it. Crowdfunding platforms have created a similar level of trust. The platform is polished and professional looking, and people trust that when they press the Pledge button, they're in good hands.

10. **It's a lot of fun** Running a crowdfunding campaign is thrilling. I don't think anything else out there is quite like it. Don't get me wrong—it's extremely stressful, but it's also a lot of fun.

I've intentionally placed these lists early in the book because this is the moment when you need to decide whether crowdfunding your dream project is worth the long hours; the limited, short-term profits; the creation of a lasting business; and engagement with hundreds or thousands of strangers.

If that's the value you place on your dream project, keep reading. If not, that's okay too—the world needs passionate consumers as much as it needs creators. There are other books out there that you can read instead. I recommend *Ready Player One* by Ernest Cline.[2]

The Evolution of Creation

Prior to the inception of Kickstarter and other crowdfunding sites, there were a few ways to raise money for a new product or service. You could ask the bank for a loan, appeal to friends or family for seed money, or compel angel investors to buy a share of your company.

There is nothing wrong with any of those methods. However, as I mentioned in the previous chapter, creating something new is about a lot more than just money. That's where Kickstarter and other crowdfunding platforms added a whole new element to project creation and funding.

Kickstarter.com went live on April 28, 2009, with a simple concept: Compose a project page about something you want to create, designate the amount you need to create it and a time frame to raise those funds, and list tangible or digital rewards that supporters ("backers") would receive if you reach the funding goal. If you don't reach the goal, no one—neither the creator nor the backers—pay Kickstarter a dime.

Thus crowdfunding was born.

Crowdfunding democratized creativity. It provided a platform for people to vote with their money on the things they want. Kickstarter gave backers a reason to share projects with their friends—if you want what you're backing to exist, you can't be the only one backing it. When you backed a Kickstarter project, you felt like you were backing a person, not a thing. And it gave backers a chance to hear the stories the crowdfunders wanted to tell about their passions, their lives, and their creations.

Now, that was back in 2009. Things have changed quite a bit since then. Established companies have started using crowdfunding to launch new products—products that would have existed regardless of successfully funding. Sometimes it feels as though you're preordering a product online instead of supporting an individual with a passion project. Many backers don't mind this as long as they're getting something cool in return for their pledge.

You can now choose from hundreds of different crowdfunding websites. Here are some of the key platforms to consider. (Keep in mind that these platforms continue to evolve, so the features I list may have changed by the time you read this.)

Kickstarter

At less than a decade old, Kickstarter is the granddaddy of crowd-funding sites. It has a clean design, a number of systems in place to help people who browse the site discover new projects, and it's easy for creators to use. One of my favorite things about Kickstarter is that it's an all-or-nothing endeavor—if you don't reach your funding goal, no credit cards are charged, and you don't receive any funds. This gives projects an important element of urgency and community because all backers are working together to achieve a common goal.

Indiegogo

Indiegogo allows pretty much any type of project, including "fund your life" projects and charity projects. It offers a "flexible funding" option that charges supporters' credit cards at the point of pledge even before you have reached your goal. Indiegogo also allows creators to move a featured reward level to the top of the reward sidebar, a small innovation that I'm a big fan of.

GoFundMe

GoFundMe allows any type of project. Like Indiegogo, creators keep all pledges (the site uses the term "donations") you receive, and you don't even have to set a time frame. GoFundMe projects don't involve rewards for supporters. My favorite aspect of GoFundMe is that creators can post a project widget on their own website and accept pledges directly through that widget.

Patreon

Most of the sites on this list are ideal for people trying to create something new. Patreon, though, is geared toward creators who want to raise money to continue making content they already produce on a regular basis. Patreon charges credit cards in small increments on an ongoing basis. For example, the producers of a podcast might use Patreon as a way for their listeners to contribute $1 per month to pay for software expenses. For a great example of a Patreon campaign, see the Secret Cabal Gaming Podcast (as of May 2015, the campaign has 226 patrons paying a total of $547.27 per episode).[3]

Crowdrise

Crowdrise is specifically a fundraising site for causes and charities. Projects can have goals, but it's not required, nor do campaigns have to stop accepting donations after the time frame ends. Creators keep all funds, even if the goal isn't reached. Like GoFundMe, Crowdrise projects don't offer rewards for supporters.

Quirky

If you have a great idea for a product but don't know how to design or manufacture it, Quirky is the site for you. People can propose an idea, vote on other ideas, and influence the design, all the while earning a stake in the future revenues of the product (which, if selected, Quirky's team will manufacture and sell).

Ulule

Ulule is essentially the Kickstarter of Europe (though Kickstarter continues to establish itself in countries outside the United States). A nice touch is that on Ulule, creators can select a custom background image for the entire project page.

Tilt

Tilt's name refers to the tipping point—just like with Kickstarter, if you don't reach your funding goal on Tilt, no credit cards are charged. A few differentiating factors for Tilt are its low fees for creators (free or 2.5 percent, compared with 8–10 percent for other sites) and the flexibility to change deadlines while the project is live.

Pozible

Pozible is kind of a mashup between Kickstarter and Patreon. It's a platform for both one-time pledges and creations as well as ongoing pledges and rewards (more of a subscription model). It has a flexible payment system and (as of May 2015) boasts a 57 percent project success rate, higher than any of the other major platforms.

Crowdfunder

All of the other examples are reward-based or charitable crowdfunding, but Crowdfunder offers equity-based crowdfunding. The site allows for anyone to be an angel investor in a startup. Because of this, the minimum pledge levels are usually quite high on Crowdfunder (several thousands of dollars).

This book focuses on reward-based crowdfunding—that is, projects where backers get something in exchange for their pledge (usually the product the creator is attempting to make).

Failure Comes First

Before I learned how to succeed in the world of crowdfunding and entrepreneurism, I had to learn how to fail. And I failed hard with the first entrepreneurial idea I pursued as an adult, TypeTribe.

TypeTribe was a web-based platform for authors to connect with readers. If you wrote something and wanted immediate feedback, you could post your work to TypeTribe for a nominal fee, and that fee would be split among anyone who read your work and gave you feedback within a twenty-four-hour period. If people didn't give constructive feedback, you could give them a low rating, and in the future only readers with high ratings would get the chance to read your work. It was essentially TaskRabbit for beta readers.

Twitter was in its infancy back then, but I started talking up the idea there, and a few hundred people signed up to be notified when TypeTribe launched. I was pretty excited. All I needed was a database-driven web application. No problem, except for one tiny thing: I'm not a software developer.

Fortunately, I found an old college friend who said he could give it a shot. We worked out a deal, and I hustled to raise the money. I had a steady job, but I didn't want to risk my savings on something that might not work. Crowdfunding didn't exist back then.

So I turned to family and friends. I wrote personal letters to my extended family explaining the idea and that I was looking for a zero-interest loan to fund the website. I was pleasantly surprised that I was able to raise $5,000 from those letters. Part of the reason I could raise this money is that I have a very supportive (and large) extended family. Another factor was that I didn't ask for much—really, I would have accepted anything. I would later apply those lessons to crowdfunding: asking for a little money from a lot of people can be more effective than asking for a lot of money from a few people.

This is where the story should take off, right? This is the part where I say that the site went live a few months later, the servers crashed because of the influx of users, we got the site working again, and soon attracted major angel investors who invited us to parties with Kanye West and Patrick Rothfuss.

Instead, nothing ever happened. My software developer ran into some programming hurdles, and eventually we parted ways. I paid back the loans to my family members and thanked them for the opportunity. It was disappointing, but as I reflected on the experience, I realized that the real reason TypeTribe never happened wasn't the lack of a website. Rather, it was that I fell in love with an idea that no one else really cared about. I realized that I needed to develop a better sense of awareness so that I could determine the difference between something I really want and something other people really want without letting my desire cloud my perception.

Crowdfunding is a huge asset for gauging demand. When you launch your crowdfunding campaign, you're going to find out whether you're the only one in love with your idea. Sometimes an idea can lead to failure. Other times it can lead to successful funding or even launch a new, energizing career.

The Gatekeepers of Creations Past

The best part of crowdfunding is that you have direct access to the crowd. The crowd is the new gatekeeper. Not your friends and family, not an angel investor, and not a bottom-line, profit-driven corporation.

Whether you're a game designer, a writer, an artist, a filmmaker, or another sort of creator, there are traditional ways to share your work with the world. Most of them involve gatekeepers, like publishers, literary agents, galleries, and television networks. Gatekeepers are important. In a sea of options, they narrow down the field to the best. But now there's a new gatekeeper in town: the crowd.

Who cares if twenty literary agents reject your novel but fifty thousand people buy it on Amazon and love it? Who cares if your painting "isn't a good fit" for local galleries but it attracts hundreds of people to your own art show? Who cares if a producer doesn't think your television program will succeed but it gets a hundred thousand views on YouTube? The only thing that matters is the crowd.

I could have designed and submitted a game to a game-publishing company. There are a number of benefits to doing that: Publishers have budgets, sales teams, convention support, artists, and way more resources and experience than a random game designer. They take care of business so that you can focus on what you love: designing games.

I get that. I respect the model, and it's great to see traditional game-publishing companies flourish. But I'm more than a game designer. I genuinely enjoy running a business — I love the puzzle of logistics, customer service, marketing, and so on. I've always wanted to apply my entrepreneurial spirit to a business of my own.

Handing off my game to a publisher didn't excite me. But putting it on Kickstarter and building something together with backers — that got my juices flowing.

Why Are You Reading This?

Simon Sinek, author of *Start with Why*, repeatedly says in his book and his very popular TEDTalk,[4] "People don't buy what you do, they buy why you do it."

Every great crowdfunder — every great *leader*, for that matter — must have a clear vision of why they do what they do. You want to be a crowdfunding creator. Why? Are you doing it for the money? For recognition? For power? For popularity? Those motivations won't attract people, nor will you be able to sustain all of the responsibilities that come with being a crowdfunder if those are your reasons for creating a project.

A seemingly more appealing motivation might be because you're trying to make your dream a reality. That's great — I love to see people make their dreams come true through crowdfunding. But that motivation is all about *you*. If that's the main reason you're interested in crowdfunding, you're probably not going to succeed. The only people who really care about your dreams are your friends and family, who will contribute about 10 percent of your funding at most.

So really, why are you here? Why are you considering crowdfunding to launch your product or company? Why are you trying to bring your idea to reality? What is it about your idea and the way you want to create it that brought you to crowdfunding? Your reasons might be very specific to your project, but in some way they should be tied to engaging people, forging relationships, and building a community through crowdfunding.

I'm not saying this because I think you should adopt my personal philosophy. I'm saying this because you will *significantly increase your chances of crowdfunding success* if your clear vision about why you're doing it is directly related to your backers. Not the money, not you, but the backers themselves.

So before you turn the page, ask yourself, "Why am I reading this book?"

CHAPTER 3

Crowdfunding Is the Rock Concert for Entrepreneurs

You never forget the first crowdfunding project you support.

I backed my first campaign on October 23, 2009. It was called "Robin Writes a Book (and you get a copy)." Compared with today's mammoth crowdfunding campaigns, Robin Writes a Book was a no-frills project. The project page itself consisted of eleven paragraphs of text and no images. There were seven reward levels, most of which involved one or more copies of the book. The funding goal was a modest $3,500, and Robin raised $13,942 from 570 backers over a two-month period.

At the time, I had no idea that Robin's campaign would inspire me to start a company, create a crowdfunding campaign, and launch a new career. All I knew was that when I pressed that Pledge button, something special happened. I felt something different from all of the hundreds of times I pressed Buy Now while shopping on the Internet.

It felt . . . magical.

I didn't know Robin Sloan, nor was I aware of his previous writing (he wrote for a website called Snarkmarket). As with many projects, I simply stumbled upon his while browsing Kickstarter's website. A few elements drew me in and motivated me to become a backer right away.

First was the project video. Robin's video is the right mix of polished, personal, and a little quirkiness. He looks at the camera as though he's speaking directly to you. The audio and video quality are great, and you can tell that Robin is really excited about the project—his enthusiasm is contagious.

Second were the reward levels. For $11, you got a book—a physical paperback book shipped to your front door at no additional cost. That's a fantastic value.

Next was the demonstration of ability and competency. Getting a great deal doesn't mean anything if the product sucks. Robin was an unknown entity to me, but he demonstrated his writing ability by sharing a link to one of his short stories on the project page.

Last, the project was already funded. Robin already had a following when he launched, allowing him to quickly fund the project. Thus, by the time I discovered it, I knew it was really going to happen and that this was something people wanted. It's like deciding between two restaurants, one with a long line and another that is almost empty. The perceived value of the restaurant with the line is much higher than for the empty one.

The most exciting element of Robin's project was that he was writing the book *during the campaign,* with a goal to complete the first draft by the end of the campaign. This captured my attention because I felt like I was part of something exciting that was happening right now. Robin aided this feeling by keeping backers in the loop through his project updates during the campaign.

This isn't a strategy I would recommend to most project creators. When a backer sees an incomplete product, they anticipate a long cycle of delays and scheduling issues. However, no matter how complete the product is, every crowdfunding campaign puts the spotlight on the creator for a short, intense period of time. It's one of the few opportunities for entrepreneurs to feel like rock stars. You're on "stage" for about thirty days, with all eyes on you as you try to deliver the best possible experience for the crowd.

My First Kickstarter As a Creator

During his campaign, Robin talked a lot about how this might be a new model of publishing books—real-time writing funded by people who wanted a copy. It was then that I really started thinking about what the future of publishing looked like.

I was in a writers group at the time, and I started talking with a few of the group's members about publishing. As it turned out, two writers who were married to each other—Jason and Kristy Makansi—were just as interested in testing the market as I was. So in January 2010, we formed a company called Blank Slate Press.

The idea behind Blank Slate Press was to focus on discovering and publishing work of local novelists. We wanted to be very selective and focus on only a few authors. It was also important that we stay small and nimble because we wanted to be able to experiment with a number of ideas for sharing our authors with the world.

Over time we signed two authors. We tried various methods of marketing our authors with mixed success, but the idea of using Kickstarter as a promotion platform stayed with me. I was ready to try a campaign for Blank Slate Press. Here is a truncated version of the project page I created:

Propel Two Authors toward the Future of Publishing

Blank Slate Press, a small indie publishing startup in St. Louis, is ready to sign two new authors to join our team. Are you in?

Hello! Thanks for visiting Blank Slate Press's debut Kickstarter campaign.

We've spent many a day discussing the pricing of our books. We've also spent many a day figuring out how to get people to spread the word about our books. That's the goal, right? You can publish the most brilliant book in the world, but if no one hears about it, you've done a disservice to the author and to the readers who missed out.

What we've realized is that there might be an intersection between pricing and spreadability (the impact on a product being shared online). Hence this experiment on Kickstarter.

Unlike most Kickstarter campaigns, all of our rewards are the same—you get digital copies of both of our books in any e-book format. However, your price depends on how much you spread the word about this campaign, Blank Slate Press, and the books themselves. A reduction in price is our way of thanking you for sharing us with your social networks.

So, for example, if you're willing to pledge to "Like," tweet, and/or e-mail the campaign to a friend, "Like" BSP on Facebook, and subscribe to BSP's monthly e-newsletter, you get our first two novels for only $4.[1] We trust you to follow through on your pledge.

The campaign ran for thirty days, starting on June 1, 2011. Twenty-eight days in, we had raised only $125. A few generous pledges over the final two days brought the funding total to $305 from seventeen backers, surpassing our goal of $250 and technically making the campaign "successful"—but it certainly didn't feel that way. I made a few mistakes with that first campaign. Big mistakes. Despite watching and studying Kickstarter for two years, I fundamentally misunderstood the purpose and function of crowdfunding.

First, I depended on the crowdfunding platform to *promote* my project. A significant part of my plan for the project was to make the project unique enough that Kickstarter would discover it and promote it. I had seen this happen with a project called The Cosmonaut ($134,236 raised from 6,192 backers). The creators, Dan Provost and Tom Gerhardt of Studio Neat, used a unique "pay what you wish" pricing scheme, and Kickstarter promoted it all over the place. So I concocted what I thought was a unique reward model involving social networking, and I sat back and waited for Kickstarter to discover and promote it. Yeah, that didn't happen, nor should I have expected it to happen. It's my job to share the project, not Kickstarter's.

Second, I depended on the crowdfunding platform for people to *discover* the project. I had stumbled upon Robin Writes a Book, so I thought that people were likely to find our campaign while browsing Kickstarter. I think only one or two of our seventeen backers discovered the project this way. The rest were friends of mine or people who knew me through my personal blog.

Third, I tried to fund something that already existed instead of seeking funding for something new. This is the core of what crowdfunding is, and it's what backers respond to so well. With Robin Writes a Book, I felt like I was part of the journey of Robin writing a book. But with the Blank Slate Press campaign, it was abundantly clear from the project video that the books already existed. We were essentially just asking people to buy the books. I've seen more and more companies try to use crowdfunding in this way to varying degrees of success, but only a few of those campaigns come close to the success of projects where the money is truly needed to make something happen. Backers respond to need.

Better Ways to Begin

The method of sharing-based currency that Blank Slate Press used didn't take off, but as Robin Sloan demonstrated, it's possible to capture the attention of an audience with some innovative approaches to crowdfunding.

One of my favorite innovative crowdfunding stories involves a crowdfunder named John Wrot. John is a gamer, a family man, and the owner of Gate Keeper Games. He's also one of the most enthusiastic, energetic people you'll ever meet. When I met John at Gen Con, a big gaming convention in Indianapolis (in fact, the biggest gaming convention in the United States), he had an exclamation mark printed on his name tag: "John Wrot!" It wasn't a typo—it's how John writes his name.

One of John's passions is game design. In July 2013, he launched a forty-day campaign for his game, The King's Armory. Unfortunately, John's enthusiasm didn't translate into success. With a core reward level of $49 and an overall funding goal of $72,000, his campaign reached only $25,279 (362 backers) when time expired.

That didn't stop John from trying again. But before he did, he used the feedback from an open discussion on BoardGameGeek to learn about what he needed to do to succeed the second time around. One of the major takeaways was that The King's Armory needed better art. But after the first campaign, John didn't have many funds in reserve to hire new artists and graphic designers. This is when John attempted a strategy I had never seen before.

Before returning to Kickstarter, John took a detour to another crowdfunding site, Indiegogo. He created a minicampaign—with a $3,500 goal—to raise money for art and graphic design.[2] It wasn't a project to fund the game itself; rather, it was specifically focused on the art.

John reached out to backers of his previous Kickstarter campaign (you can still post updates if you don't reach your funding goal or even if you cancel your project) to tell them about the Indiegogo project. Sixty-six of his most passionate backers responded and became Indiegogo "funders," the vast majority of whom chose digital goals or credits toward shipping on the ensuing Kickstarter project so that John could focus all of the funds on the art. The minicampaign was a success, raising $3,774.

The refined illustrations paid off in spades, as did John's

continued commitment to open communication with his original backers. When John relaunched The King's Armory on October 28, 2013, he raised more than $20,000 toward his new funding goal ($49,000 compared with the original goal of $72,000) on the first day. After thirty days (compared with forty on the original campaign), The King's Armory was substantially overfunded, with $90,389 from 815 backers.

Minicampaigns

After I learned about John's minicampaign and how it propelled his relaunched project to success, I went searching for other minicampaigns. I found one other example with a slightly different take on the strategy.

While they were preparing to put a card game called Two Rooms and a Boom on Kickstarter, Alan Gerding and Sean McCoy of Tuesday Night Games came up with a zany idea: why not document the process by funding a film about Kickstarting tabletop games . . . on Kickstarter?

One month later, they had raised $4,550 (compared with a $2,200 goal) from 113 backers on the Boom or Doom! Kickstarter Adventures in the Tabletop World project.[3] Here's Sean and Alan on why they tried this and how it worked out:[4]

> SEAN: The minicampaign and the documentary were entirely Alan's idea. I wasn't a huge fan of it at first; I wanted to put all our resources behind the Two Rooms KS. I'm insanely glad we did it, though. There's just some lessons you won't learn until you hit that Launch button. You don't know what information you'll have on the back end. You don't know what it's going to feel like to get a backer. You haven't thought of what messages you'll need to send out. You haven't thought

about graphics for updates—there's just a whole lot that you're blind to. For us, it was a chance to get a game in the win column early on with a successfully funded Kickstarter campaign, to know what we were getting into.

ALAN: Many of our backers were friends and family. But many other backers were some bigger names in the gaming industry. The beauty of the documentary is that it gave us a concrete excuse to approach Justin Gary, Michael Mindes, Cory Jones, and so many other successful Kickstarters in the industry and interview them for advice. So not only did the documentary gives us an educational experience about Kickstarter, but it also was like a "back-stage pass" at Gen Con.

Instead of starting out with their dream project, Sean and Alan used the film campaign to help get their feet wet in the world of crowdfunding. When they launched the campaign for the game itself one month later (Two Rooms and a Boom!),[5] it was a resounding hit, raising $102,102 (with a $10,000 goal) from 3,863 backers.

Humble Campaigns

A "humble campaign" is very similar to Sean and Alan's approach: launch a small campaign as your first project to learn the ropes, then launch a more ambitious project later. Humble campaigns aren't meant to raise $100,000+ from thousands of backers, though. They have humble ambitions. Not only is this good for running the campaign itself, but it also gives you the opportunity to learn how to create and ship something without the pressure of thousands of backers. The other benefit of a humble campaign is that it's not as all consuming as a big, complex project. You might actually get to sleep and eat on a regular schedule during a humble campaign.

A prime example of a humble campaign is Michael Iachini's

light card game, Otters. In a postmortem blog post[6] following his successful campaign ($5,321 raised from 246 backers), Michael outlined the five core elements of a humble campaign:

- **Low funding goal**   Keep the product simple and find a way to produce it in small print runs.

- **Paid graphic design**   Just because a campaign is humble doesn't mean it shouldn't look polished and professional.

- **Creative Commons art**   The cards in Otters feature photos of actual otters downloaded from Google Images using a filter for images that are available for reuse (even for commercial purposes, pending credit to the photographers).

- **Efficient marketing**   Instead of spending every waking hour on social media, Michael targeted specific reviewers and offered them prototype copies of Otters before the campaign. All he had to do during the campaign was share the reviews when they went live.

- **Limited expandability**   Michael offered exactly two stretch goals (compared with dozens for many other projects) and one add-on. In doing so, he intentionally limited the growth potential for the project.

You might read this and wonder why you would want to run a humble campaign for $12K or $5K when you create something that could raise $100K. Aside from the standard cautionary tales about letting a project spiral out of control, maintaining a manageable project is like having a summer internship before jumping into a career at an unknown organization. It gives you the chance to poke around, experience the pros and cons firsthand, and make a few mistakes without jeopardizing your entire future.

Micropricing

Micropricing is a prime example of how going small can have big results.

Tasty Minstrel Games, run by Michael Mindes (mentioned earlier for creating the concept of stretch goals on Kickstarter), is the master of micropricing. The idea is to create a no-brainer price for a product to bring in a ton of backers even if your margins are slim, creating a user base to leverage in the future.

Michael fully embraced this concept for the first time on Dungeon Roll,[7] a $15 game on Kickstarter with a $15,000 goal. It was a legendary campaign in the board-game industry, as it ended up raising $250,070. As impressive as that funding amount is, the more important number is the number of backers: 10,877. That's a *lot* of people to add to an e-newsletter list (even if not everyone opts in). At the time, Dungeon Roll held the record for the most backers on a tabletop game Kickstarter project.

One other example of micropricing is a campaign for a smartphone app called 1 Second Everyday by Cesar Kuriyama.[8] Cesar's app lets users capture one second of video every day and splice together those seconds over months or even years to create a seamless video that feels like a mix of a memory and a dream. In Cesar's words on the project page:

> **On the day I turned 30 years old, I started recording 1 second every day for the rest of my life** ... and I think you should too. When I turn 40, I'll have a 1-hour video that encapsulates my 30s. If I live to see 80 years of age, I'll have a 5-hour video that summarizes 50 years of my life.

Aside from developing the app itself, Cesar did something both truly brilliant and blindingly obvious with his campaign pricing: the pledge for the app was $1. Not $3. Not $5. Not $10. Just $1. The standard price for a mobile app.

A lot of campaigns would have charged more, but Cesar knew that people were already trained by Apple to purchase 99 cent apps without thinking twice about it. It's a no-brainer price. For people who wanted to pay a little more to support Cesar's passion, he included a $5 pledge level for pretty much the same thing (plus your name in the credits of the app).

The strategy reaped huge rewards, with the campaign earning $56,959 from a whopping 11,281 backers.

For the right product, consider micropricing as a strategy to attract a huge number of backers and create a solid foundation for your company's future.

Pay What You Wish

A slight twist on the micropricing method is the pay-what-you-wish model I mentioned earlier in connection to Studio Neat and the Cosmonaut. Michael took a similar approach with a very small card and coin game called Coin Age.[9] At a minimum pledge level of $3, backers could pledge any amount they wanted (suggested price: $5). Coin Age raised $65,195 from 9,055 backers—again, Michael was working to build an audience.

The pay-what-you-wish model comes with some built-in risk. It's not ideal for products that cost a lot to produce or ship, as some backers will pay only the bare minimum, potentially causing the creator a net loss. Patrick Nickel of Crash Games explored the concept with that possibility in mind on his Where Art Thou, Romeo Kickstarter project in December 2013.[10] The core reward level was $1, and backers could pledge any amount they wanted. It successfully funded at a total of $5,723.

Patrick shared some data from the project on his blog a few months later.[11] The total cost to manufacture and ship the game (which consisted of five cards, a small rule book, and a plastic bag) was $1.60 within the United States. US backers pledged an average of $2.07 for the game.

So the net gain was minimal, but the long-term addition of 2,188 backers (many of them new to Crash Games projects) was a huge boon for the company. It was a win-win for both backers and creator: backers got a game at the price that felt right to them, and Patrick got the attention of thousands of people. Patrick told me that he saw an immediate impact on the sales of a related—and more expensive—game, Council of Verona.

I realized through the Blank Slate Press project and by researching other innovative campaigns that I still had a ton to learn about crowdfunding. I wanted a second chance at a crowdfunding project. Most of all, I wanted to create something of my own with the support of people who shared my passion.

CHAPTER 4

I Made These Mistakes So You Don't Have To

I've made a *lot* of crowdfunding mistakes.

This chapter touches on some of the boneheaded things I've done as a creator, but I'm not alone—I see a lot of the same missteps on crowdfunding projects. You can increase your own chances of success by avoiding the same mistakes.

Top Ten Most Common Crowdfunding Mistakes

1. **Launching without a crowd**   The creator has neither built a community in advance of the project nor has backed and participated in at least ten to twenty projects.

2. **Minimal conversation**   The creator does not actively engage his or her backers during the campaign through comments, project updates, and polls.

3. **Poor demonstration**   The creator uses bad art, low-quality graphic design, and a project page that doesn't clearly convey what the product is or why the creator is excited about it.

4. **Unappealing reward structure**   Rewards are disproportionately expensive compared with their perceived value, pledge levels are diluted by rewards unrelated to the core product (such as T-shirts, coffee mugs, and so on), and the presence of early-bird rewards separates backers into winners (the minority) and losers (the majority).

5. **Expensive shipping rates**   Worldwide shipping fees are priced too high, and products do not ship from within key regions (like Canada, Australia, or the EU), resulting in customs fees and taxes for backers.

6. **Inaccurate funding goal**   The goal is either too high for backers to believe the project will fund or too low for backers to trust that the creator can accomplish her goals on such a limited budget.

7. **Pushy promotional approach**   The creator spams social media to promote his project and constantly badgers backers to do the same. The creator also includes exclusive content in the project rewards that forces backers to fear they are missing out instead of focusing on the many other appealing ways they are made to feel welcome.

8. **Uninspired and unvetted product**   The project does not highlight unique elements of the product, and third-party reviewers haven't vetted the product (which should be finished enough for other people to review).

9. **Too many project updates**   More than three or four updates a week during the campaign will cause backers to unsubscribe in droves.

10. **Everything is too long**   The duration of the project is too long (more than thirty-five days) and thus lacks urgency; the project page is filled with lengthy information that could be condensed; the project video is more than two minutes.

The Art and Science of Making Wine

By October 2011, some time had passed since I had tried to design a board game. Up until that point I didn't imagine that anyone would want to play a board game I designed, much less buy one. There were already so many published games on the market.

But I started to get a creative itch, and in the back of my head I thought that using a crowdfunding project as motivation might scratch it. A few board-game projects had started popping up with some success on Kickstarter—Alien Frontiers ($14,885 raised from 228 backers), Eminent Domain ($48,378 raised from 699 backers), and Rise! ($17,518 raised from 410 backers) among them—which was enough evidence to motivate me to start toying around with a game concept.

When I set out to design the game, I wasn't designing just any game . . . I was designing a game *to crowdfund*. Specifically, I wanted to engage and connect with lots of people directly through crowdfunding. I wanted to build a community of gamers and nongamers alike, so the theme of the game was really important. As much as I love wizards, dragons, and futuristic space adventures, I thought those themes might be turnoffs for nongamers.

That's when I came up with the winemaking theme. I'm not a huge wine drinker, but the romanticized idea of owning a vineyard appeals to me. I like the cycle of planting vines in the spring based on clever calculations of sun and soil, cutting fresh wood to build trellises in the summer, picking grapes off the field in the fall, and creating interesting types of wine in the winter. So I decided to make a winemaking game.

I worked on Viticulture (fig. 3), as the game came to be known, for about a month on pen and paper before it hit the table for the first time. It was then that I learned something that I had missed when designing games as a kid: when you play your game with real people for the first time, it will be completely different from how you envisioned it in your mind.

I'm really glad I discovered this early on, and it's important for all creators to know. Let other people experience your work *before*

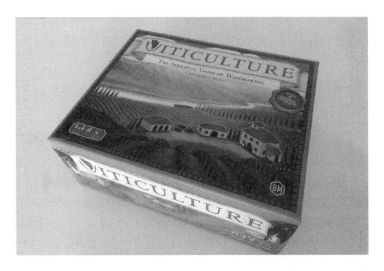

FIGURE 3. The box for Viticulture: The Strategic Game of Winemaking.

you crowdfund it. For a game, this means sharing the rules and the prototype files online as well as playtesting the game at conventions and meetups. Not only will sharing your game in this way improve your work, but it could save you a lot of time if your work turns out to completely suck and you should refocus your energy on something better. Don't worry about people stealing your idea. Worry more about turning your idea into something real and awesome.

The Turning Point

So over the next month or two, I would playtest the game, use that feedback to improve the design, and then playtest it with a different group. Rinse, repeat. The most pivotal of these playtests was with my friend Alan Stone and his wife, Erin. We played Viticulture a few times, they gave me feedback, and I went home to my cats. It seemed like any other playtest.

The next day I got a call from Alan. "I really like where Viticulture is headed," he said. "I've been talking to Erin for a while about designing a game or making *something*. I have this itch to create, but I can't do it alone. Would you consider taking on a business partner to develop Viticulture?" '

This was one of the best phone calls I've ever received.

You see, I like working alone. I like creating alone. Although I've come to appreciate the power of brainstorming, I'm perfectly happy sitting at my desk for hours and writing, designing, revising, and the like.

But I was starting to realize with Viticulture that developing a game is a lonely and difficult endeavor to take on by yourself. You're constantly asking for your friends' time to playtest a game that probably isn't very good at that point. They would prefer to play real, polished, published games. In a way, it's the same issue that drove the creation of TypeTribe—I wanted people to read my short stories, but I didn't want to impose upon my friends.

Thus, having Alan say that he *wanted* to develop Viticulture with me was a huge boost. Even though I run Stonemaier Games, the company and our games would not exist without Alan.

Going in Blind

In February 2012, I mocked up a prototype to send out for blind playtesting—that's when people play a game without you there to explain the rules. At the time, I had started to run the costs for producing Viticulture en masse. I had yet another huge misconception about crowdfunding projects: I saw them as homegrown efforts that require the creators to do everything by hand, like Tyler Durden making soap in the kitchen in *Fight Club*. I foresaw Alan and me printing out thousands of cards at our local copier, sorting them for each game, hand packing the game, and shipping copies out one by one.

The truth is, the best way to share your creativity with the world is to find a way to do it at various scales. Sure, if only ten people are interested in your work, make it by hand, and make it really special. But if a hundred or a thousand people want your creation, you better be prepared for it. It's not fair to those people if you make something half-assed just because you couldn't figure out how proper manufacturing and fulfillment works.

After creating prototypes by hand for a mere ten games, we realized that wasn't sustainable in terms of time, money, or energy. They also looked terrible. We had to find an alternative to mass-producing Viticulture in my living room or we were never going to be able to publish the game.

The Panda in the Room

The biggest assets for my crowdfunding research were other board-game Kickstarter projects. I created a giant spreadsheet of projects I admired, looking for patterns between reward pricing, project structure, and manufacturing. The more great projects I looked at, the more I realized that one manufacturing company was rising above the rest: Panda Game Manufacturing.

Panda was founded by two Canadian brothers, Michael and Richard Lee. They grew up playing tabletop games, and when Michael was looking for some business opportunities in his late twenties, he noticed a lack of game manufacturers that could produce small print runs at reasonable prices. At the time, a few of the big game-publishing companies owned manufacturing facilities (mostly in Germany), and US factories weren't set up to produce the small, precise pieces that many games require, especially not at a low cost for small print runs.

So Michael turned to China, and he did so in a very clever way. He didn't set out to open a factory that could produce any component for any game. Other factories across China already had the capacity to manufacture specific types of components. Michael vetted those factories and found the best one of each type. He also formed a joint venture with a facility in Shenzhen, which became the home to their overseas management team, printing operation, and quality-control team.

The most important aspect of Panda for any independent game company, particularly one that uses Kickstarter, is one number: 1,500. Fifteen hundred is the minimum number of games Panda can produce. This may seem like a lot, but in terms of the greater game industry, it's not much at all. Try asking other manufacturers to make 1,500 of something for you. They're much more likely to give you a minimum of 5,000 or 10,000.

Having a minimum of 1,500 is so important because it lets you budget for a specific funding goal. You need to raise enough money to make 1,500 games, ship individual games to each backer, and send the rest of the games to distributors to sell to online and brick-and-mortar retailers (in the game industry, we call them FLGS—Friendly Local Game Stores). Your budget depends on that number, as does your funding goal.

Around June 2012, with Panda's preliminary estimate in hand, I met with Alan to discuss the next step for Viticulture. We knew we wanted to use Kickstarter to fund it, but we also knew that we would have some upfront costs to cover for art, design, and review prototypes so that we could position Viticulture as an attractive option for Kickstarter browsers. It turned out to be a fateful meeting because its results—as well as several missteps that followed—should have, by anyone's estimation, brought an early end to Viticulture and Stonemaier Games.

A Brief History of Near Failure

When I look back at the Viticulture Kickstarter campaign and compare it with successful campaigns today, I'm surprised it successfully funded (and I'm grateful that my backers took a chance on me). I made a lot of bad decisions for the campaign, the game, and Stonemaier Games, and I have no doubt in my mind that those decisions negatively affected the campaign. Here's an account of those mistakes so that other project creators can avoid them.

Misaligned Expectations in Partnerships

When Alan Stone and I met in July 2012 to discuss ways to finance upfront, pre-Kickstarter costs for Viticulture, we decided to take on two partners. The idea was a good one: spread out the costs to a few other people who believe in what we're doing, partially removing the financial burden from us if the Kickstarter project failed. Also, we wanted to create a team of people with talents and skills that Alan and I didn't possess.

Our partners had the best of intentions, and to this day I'm grateful to them for taking a risk on us. They had financial means that Alan and I didn't have access to, and they were well connected with many of the wineries in the area. All four of us invested a small amount of money in the company to pay for some basic art, design, and ads on BoardGameGeek, a website geared toward gamers, and we split the ownership of Stonemaier Games into thirds: 33 percent for me, 33 percent for Alan, and 33 percent for the final two partners.

However, there was some confusion about each of our responsibilities as partners, and it quickly became apparent that the 33 percent split didn't accurately represent the true division of labor. This was largely my fault—knowing how much time I was going to spend on Viticulture, I should have asked for a larger percentage of the company from the beginning, but I wanted to respect the fact that we were all injecting the same amount of money into Stonemaier.

Unfortunately, despite our plan, my partners didn't execute their responsibilities to the company during the campaign, at least not to the extent I expected. I wasn't as clear as I should have been, not just in terms of *what* our responsibilities were, but also *why* we had those responsibilities.

Stonemaier Games has changed and grown a lot since that original campaign, and part of that evolution was a restructuring to accurately reflect the effort we were each putting into the company. Now it's just Alan and me as partners and owners of the company. I run the day-to-day operations as my full-time job, and Alan helps out with specific tasks on a part-time basis.

What we should have done   Running a Kickstarter project means you need to be a leader. Great leaders clearly communicate their expectations. I should have explained everyone's responsibilities before the partnership was formed and on an ongoing basis afterward.

Going Cheap on Art and Design

One of the biggest mistakes I try to prevent other creators from making is having subpar art and graphic design for their crowdfunding project, yet it's a mistake I made myself with Viticulture.

Artists can be quite expensive. We had a limited preproject budget, so I did what many project creators do and will continue to do: I turned to a friend to get a good deal. This is a terrible idea. Not because your friends aren't great—I'm sure they are. But because they're your friends, you're already biased about their work. You *want* to like their work, and therefore you're not looking at it through the same lens you would if you hired a professional to produce the best possible art. Also, you figure you'll get a good deal, which further influences your perception.

The artist I originally hired for Viticulture is extremely talented. The problem is, he works primarily with paint and pencil, and the type of art used for board games is created digitally. So even though the art he created for Viticulture's game board wasn't the type of art typically used for a board game, it had a distinct look to it and certainly wasn't bad, which was probably the saving grace for the project.

Graphic design was a slightly different situation. Alan and I put together a list of three graphic designers: two friends (both professional graphic designers) and one college senior. (I worked at a university at the time, and I had commissioned some graphic design from that student in the past.)

We requested quotes from all three designers, and, of course, the college student's quote was lower than the two ten-year industry veterans. So we went with the cheapest option.

You can probably guess where this is headed. Just like the original artist, the original graphic designer is very talented. But there is only so much you can learn in school compared with the experience you gain from working at design firms and as a freelancer for a decade. The student designer's logos were great, but I wasn't pleased with the design on the game board, so at one point I sent the current versions of the files to my experienced designer friend to see what she thought. After spending ten minutes with the files, she found dozens of errors and issues with printer compatibility. I realized that I was putting the success of the project at risk for the sake of saving about $500, so I paid the student designer for her work and moved on to my professional designer friend, Christine Santana. I'm still working with Christine today.

What we should have done For our artist, we should have scoured websites like Deviant Art, Concept Art, Pinterest, and BoardGameGeek until we found artists whose work fit the theme of the game well and then obtained quotes from them. They might have been more expensive than what we were able to pay to complete the entire project, but acquiring some art for the project page should be a part of every crowdfunder's budget. For the graphic designer, we should have found a professional graphic designer specializing in print media. It's worth the money.

Not Engaging the Industry and Community before the Kickstarter Campaign

No matter what kind of project you're running, there's a community of people out there who actively discuss that category. For example, if you're trying to fund a new type of kitchen utensil, there are websites and blogs where people—chefs, moms, industrial designers—love to talk about kitchen utensils. You should be talking to those people! And I don't mean that you should be self-promoting your project to those people. I mean that you should make yourself part of that community long before your project launches—not just to make connections with those people, but to learn the ins and outs of an industry that you probably don't understand as well as you think you do.

If I could travel back to 2010, I would tell myself (a) not to ever grow my hair long (huge mistake) and (b) to be an active member on BoardGameGeek, every blog related to board games, and every YouTube channel on the topic. I would have learned so much about the board-game industry, game design, and how gamers interact with each other online. I would also have made a lot of great connections with people who probably would have backed Viticulture.

Perhaps most important, connecting with other game designers and bloggers well in advance of the Kickstarter would have given me an opportunity to help them. I'll talk about the importance of generosity in the next chapter because I think it's very important to help others before you even consider asking them to help you.

What we should have done We should have been much more active in the board-game community (online and in St. Louis) well in advance of Viticulture's launch.

Lack of Third-Party Reviews

For reasons that I cannot fathom now, I didn't reach out to third-party reviewers for Viticulture until after the Kickstarter campaign began. These days it's almost unheard of for a board-game project to succeed without third-party reviews. Keep in mind that you're asking strangers to give you money for a game that won't be delivered for six months at the very least. It's tough for them to entrust you with their money unless they've already heard from reviewers that you've created a decent game.

Plus, creating prototypes and reaching out to reviewers takes a lot of time, which is your most precious resource during a crowdfunding campaign. And it's not very respectful of a game reviewer's time to ask that he review your game within a few weeks. Give him at least a month's notice before the campaign, and get the prototype to the reviewer ASAP.

Also, and tied to the previous mistake we made, being an active participant on the reviewer's blog, podcast, or YouTube channel long before you request a review can make a big difference. Reviewers have limited time, so if they get two requests on the same day, one from someone they've never heard of and the other from someone who they recognize as a frequent commenter on their blog, guess whose request they're going to pick?

We were very fortunate with Viticulture because a number of third-party reviewers agreed to review the game during the campaign. It helped that it was a longer campaign (forty-two days) because they wouldn't have had the time to publish the reviews otherwise. (I encourage first-time project creators to schedule thirty-five-day campaigns to give them plenty of time to learn the ropes.) I'm forever grateful to GeekDad, Father Geek, Crits Happen, Dice Hate Me, and Ryan Metzler for reviewing Viticulture on such short notice.

What we should have done Just as I do now, I should have contacted third-party reviewers at least a month in advance and sent them a nice prototype of Viticulture with plenty of time to spare before we launched the campaign.

Misguided Approach to the Project Video

When I ran the Kickstarter campaign for Blank Slate Press, I made the mistake of hinging the project's success on Kickstarter noticing and promoting the project. You would think that I would learn from that lesson.

Nope! At least not for the project video.

When I was planning the project video for Viticulture, I noticed a trend on Kickstarter's "Project of the Day" e-mails about unique and funny project videos. So I decided to use the Viticulture video to spoof the trailer for the wine-country comedy *Sideways*.

Fortunately for you (but not for me), that video is now on Kickstarter forever. It's a lighthearted video about a few friends who go on a road trip and end up talking to some girls about their board game. It's fun, but it doesn't convey our passion for the game or what's unique about the game, nor does it feature many compelling visuals.

What we should have done   After running six projects and researching countless others, I've discovered a few elements that make for an effective project video.

The most effective project videos are an expression of the creator's excitement and passion. A great example of this is Luke Brown's video for The Beer Hammer project ($16,402 raised from 349 backers).[1] It runs a bit long, but by the end of it, you're fully invested in Luke's story as a self-taught carpenter in South Dakota. You'll believe in the craftsmanship of the hand-carved, beer-bottle-opening gavel after watching the video.

Compelling project videos use powerful visuals to clearly convey what the project is about. A great example of this is the project video for the documentary *Bluebird Man* ($17,241 raised from 207 backers),[2] in which the director, Neil Paprocki, demonstrates his cinematography abilities (this is obviously very important for any film project). Awesome videos serve as your "elevator pitch" to backers by sharing the most unique and interesting elements of the project. The best pitches are succinct: one to two minutes at most, plus or minus thirty seconds. Here are some statistics about my project videos:

- **Viticulture**   13,958 plays (31.85 percent of plays completed; 2:44 running time)

- **Euphoria**   24,413 plays (41.73 percent of plays completed; 2:59 running time)

- **Tuscany**   10,107 plays (34.32 percent of plays completed; 2:20 running time)

- **Treasure Chest**   13,508 plays (59.34 percent of plays completed; 0:59 running time)

- **Between Two Cities**   20,986 plays (53.38 percent of plays completed; 1:00 running time)

- **New Treasure Chests**   6,316 plays (63.95 percent of plays completed; 0:59 running time

Why the huge jump on the completed plays of the Treasure Chest and Between Two Cities videos? They were each only one minute long.

Not Following the Crowdfunding Website's Rules

Every crowdfunding platform has specific rules you need to fully understand before you launch your project. For example, Kickstarter has an extensive but very clear list of guidelines you have to follow if you want to post a project on their site. A few of the key guidelines that people often overlook are as follows (as of February 2015):

- Projects must create something to share with others.

- Every project on Kickstarter must fit into one of these categories: art, comics, crafts, dance, design, fashion, film and video, food, games, journalism, music, photography, publishing, technology, and theater.

- Projects can't fundraise for charity, offer financial incentives, or involve prohibited items. (Other crowdfunding sites, like Indiegogo, Gofundme, and Crowdrise, offer more flexibility than Kickstarter for projects like these.)

- Creators cannot offer equity or financial incentives (ownership, share of profits, repayment or loans, cash-value equivalents, etc.).

- Kickstarter cannot be used to fund software projects not run by the developers themselves.

- Projects cannot offer alcohol as a reward.

- No contests, coupons, gambling, raffles, and lifetime memberships.

Most crowdfunding websites don't require that you follow an approval process to launch your project, so violations of the site's guidelines are brought to the attention of the website only when a backer reports an issue after the project goes live.

That's exactly what happened with Viticulture, on launch day, while it was being featured on the Recently Launched section on Kickstarter.

The issue was a limited reward I offered on Viticulture that gave sixteen people a seat at a Viticulture tournament with a cash prize. I didn't think it violated Kickstarter's guidelines about offering cash as rewards or contests, and I assumed Kickstarter had seen it when they approved the project, but I've come to realize that the people who review projects can't examine every little detail of the project page. Either way, I should have checked with Kickstarter if I had any doubt.

When an anonymous backer alerted Kickstarter to the indiscretion on launch day, Kickstarter immediately removed the project from the Recently Launched page (from which we were getting a lot of backers). They were kind enough to let the project remain live while I removed the reward level, but it definitely had an impact on the project's momentum.

What we should have done   I should have read the project guidelines one more time before submitting Viticulture for approval, and if I had any doubt about any aspect of the project, I should have checked with Kickstarter first.

The combination of all of these mistakes should have spelled doom for Viticulture and Stonemaier Games. But it didn't—all because of something special that happened when I pressed the Launch button for Viticulture's Kickstarter campaign.

CHAPTER 5

Make It about Them

Sometimes you don't realize you have a personal philosophy until it shows up at your front door wearing nothing but a trench coat.

For me, the front door was my Kickstarter campaign for Viticulture. For the year leading up to the campaign, designing Viticulture was all about *me*. It was about me making a game that I wanted to play. It was about the act of creation. It was about my desire to use crowdfunding to launch something for *me*.

But the minute I pressed that Launch button, something changed. It had probably been changing for a while, but it didn't fully hit me until I launched the project. It was then that I realized I was far more interested in making something for other people than for myself. I didn't want Viticulture to be about me anymore, I wanted it to be about the people who discovered it through the crowdfunding campaign and became a part of the foundation for the game. It was about the bloggers and reviewers who took a chance on a complete unknown to offer their feedback, advice, and reviews. It was about being good and fair and responsive to people. It was about making something that would bring people together for memorable, joyful, creative moments.

My personal philosophy, I realized, was to *make it about them*.

I've had complete clarity since I had that realization. It has been the source and the guiding compass of every decision I've made for Stonemaier Games—not just for our crowdfunding campaigns and our games, but also for my blog and this book. This book isn't about me. It's about helping other creators and, I hope, making crowdfunding a better place for everyone.

Focus on the Crowd

Make it about them: Those four words embody the philosophy of everything I do as creator, entrepreneur, and president of Stonemaier Games. They're a personal choice for me, and I'm not here to convince you to adopt my philosophy. I hope you have your own philosophy or you're in the process of discovering it.

But I am here to make a proposal. I propose that the philosophy of focusing on others instead of yourself will *significantly* increase the chances of success for your crowdfunding campaign. I'll cover three target audiences to illustrate this point, each as an example of how you could make a campaign about you or make it about them.

Backers

You design a purse that's made for carrying your cat around with you, and you create a crowdfunding project for it. You then choose between two approaches:

Make It about You

The purse costs $22 to make and $10 to ship within the United States, but you price it at $70 because your goal is to make lots of money. On the project page, you talk about how important the purse is to you and how people should back the project to help you. During the campaign, some backers propose that you offer the purse in different colors to match their cats, but you tell them you're not interested in deviating from the original plan (you don't admit this, but your resistance stems from the extra work involved). Blue is *your* favorite color, so that's the only color you offer. Most of your project updates focus on asking backers to spread the word about the campaign.

Make It about Them

Set the price for the standard purse at $39, and price a premium catnip version at $49. The lower price point makes the purse far more accessible to potential backers. Focus your project page on why the purse will make people happier. Potential backers can see that you're interested in making a product for them, not just for you.

When backers propose some changes to the purse, leap at the chance to *discuss* the proposed changes. (Note the word "discuss." You can talk about your ideas with backers without compromising your vision.) You know what you want, but try to put yourself in the shoes of three to five other people. What's the ideal version of your product for them? Take it as a compliment that backers are so passionate about your purse concept that they're willing to spend the time to create new variations. Many of these backers spread the word about the revised plans for your purse because they feel like they played a role in its evolution.

Your project updates contain content that lets backers see behind the scenes of the purse's creation. You post photos of the purse with cats in it, and you link to Twitter photos of backers' cats. Instead of telling backers what they can do for you, you make the campaign a fun ride for everyone involved. In a way, you let your backers become your crowdfunding family.

Can you see the difference? Can you also see how easy it is to fall into the "make it about you" category? We've all done it. The key is to be aware of it and to see how it can hurt your chances of success.

A quote by Jason Zimdars of the Signal vs. Noise blog sums up the concept of making the project and the product about the backers instead of yourself: "Who is the star of your product? Do you want people to think your product is awesome, or would you rather they felt awesome about themselves because they used your product?"[1]

I think of that statement whenever I get caught up in thinking about how amazing one of my games is. In a vacuum, the game itself doesn't matter. What matters are the backers who swell with pride at game night when they get to pull their first-edition copy of Viticulture off the shelf and tell someone that they were there from the beginning. They *built* this game, this company. That feeling is a precious commodity unique to crowdfunding.

Readers

Building a community before a crowdfunding campaign by creating content—a blog, podcast, YouTube channel, and so on—is a key ingredient to a successful project. The way you structure your content will affect your readership and fan base.

In December 2012, I had finished previewing all of the cards in Viticulture on the Stonemaier Games blog. While it was an exciting process to share the cards with backers and readers, something felt odd about those blog entries. They seemed a bit self-centered. I was focusing on my game instead of on how I could add something of value to the world.

So I sat down at my computer and wrote an entry titled "Kickstarter Lesson #1: Starting and Submitting Your Project Page." At the time I wasn't sure where the series would lead, but I figured it was a good place to start. And it felt good to put something out there on the Internet that could help other project creators. I wish resources like that had existed when I was working on my first Kickstarter campaign. (A wish like this is, by the way, a great place to start. What resource do you wish you could have? Once you figure that out, go create that resource.)

As soon as I focused the blog on helping other people by

identifying and explaining my mistakes, insights, and research, readership skyrocketed. Within three months I had the same number of readers as for my personal blog, which I had diligently maintained for nearly six years. Thousands of people not only read the entries but also commented on them and shared them with other Kickstarter creators.

Blogging has taught me so much about engaging people, establishing my voice online, and creating content that focuses on other people's needs instead of my own. Here's what I've learned after consistently blogging over the last eight years:

Blogging taught me how to connect with people online   There are things you won't truly understand about connecting with an online audience until you do it in blog form. Kickstarter project pages and updates are very similar to blogs in terms of long-form content, so now is your time to hone those skills. For example, by writing a blog (and reading lots of blogs) you will learn that people find it much easier to read content when you use lots of lists and keep your paragraphs as short as possible. You will also learn how to respond to comments that are less than favorable.

Blogging helped me develop a readership (and a small fan base) It's a bit of a stretch to think that you will be able to convert your readers to backers. Some will support you—perhaps about 5 percent of your regular readers. That doesn't mean that a readership isn't important, though. They may not buy your product, but they may share it or simply offer words of encouragement and feedback. If you're crowdfunding a product, you need to start building that crowd well in advance of the project launch (at least six to twelve months beforehand).

A great example of this is the Exploding Kittens card game from Matthew Inman, the creator of The Oatmeal, an online comic. Since 2009, Inman has offered free content on his website to a growing number of fans. As of May 2015, The Oatmeal's Alexa rank was just over 5,000—equivalent to between seven and eight million visitors a month.

So when Inman launched a crowdfunding campaign in January 2015 with a few partners (Elan Lee and Shane Small), he already had a huge fan base. As a result, the project rocketed to success, raising $2 million in just over the first twenty-four hours.

Blogging gave me a wealth of content to share   Content is good. Content establishes an online presence, a symbol of commitment, and legitimacy. It shows transparency and wisdom, or perhaps humor and a human touch. Content gives you something to share with people and something to keep them in the loop. If you don't give strangers a reason to stay in the loop now, how are you going to get in touch with them when you have a project to share? Also, having a wealth of good content increases the chances that strangers will discover your blog via online search engines.

Blogging taught me how to express my personality online—and when to edit myself   This goes back to the concept of exposing yourself online, which I introduced in Chapter 2. I write about a broad variety of topics. Between my personal blog and my Stonemaier blog, I write about pet peeves, my greatest fears, relationships, leadership, Kickstarter, game design ... the list goes on. It's a broad list because I'm interested in a lot of things, and I don't want to pigeonhole what I write about.

But the key element that connects all of those entries is that I'm myself when I write them. I try not to write in a formal, pedantic third-party voice. It's just me having a conversation with the readers. Along the way, though, I have learned that there are certain conversations I don't want to have with readers. That is, I avoid topics that incense people. They can lead to a lot of hits and comments, but I want people to walk away after reading my blog entries feeling good, not angry. That's especially key with the "Kickstarter Lessons." If I write something that puts readers on the defensive, they're not going to take away anything of value from the entries.

Perhaps most of all, blogging has made me a more selfless person. A blog is not a diary. A diary is an outlet to say anything you want without considering other readers because you are the only reader. A blog is almost the exact opposite. If you don't consider the reader when you're writing a blog, you're missing the point—it might as well be a diary then. A blog is about creating content that engages, intrigues, amuses, and educates the reader. It's not about you. It's about the reader. It's about *them*.

In the next example, you've created a board game that you're putting on Kickstarter in a few months. You decide to write a blog, and there are two approaches you can take:

Make It about You

You define the goal of your blog as a way to promote your upcoming crowdfunding campaign. The vast majority of your blog's content is about the design of your game, without applying what you've learned to what readers can learn about game's design in general. Your blog entries include a number of references that new readers and strangers won't understand, and you rarely use paragraph breaks, lists, or images to break up large chunks of text. Some people comment on your blog entries, but you don't want to spend your time responding to comments, so you don't.

Make It about Them

Define the goal of your blog as a way to share game-design tips with other game designers. You understand that the point of your blog isn't to promote yourself and your crowdfunding campaign. Get it out of your head right now that you're here to promote something.

The content of your blog uses examples from a variety of games (including your own) to illustrate key game-design insights. You understand that no one really cares about your game yet; rather, they care about the games they already know how to play, and they don't mind the occasional reference to your game.

Keep the language of your blog as inclusive as possible. Most random readers don't know your wife's name is Susan or that your game has evolved from a worker-placement game to a card-drafting game. You get exactly one shot at a new reader, so write each entry as though the audience is new to your blog.

Recognize that reading a blog online is very different from reading a book, so break up your text into small, manageable bits: short paragraphs, lists, and images help to catch the reader's attention and maintain it.

You invite conversation by ending most entries with an open-ended question, and you are an active participant in the comments section. The blog is a platform for a discussion, not a soap box.

Subscribe to lots of blogs and pay attention to the ones that you actually read every day. Analyze why you read them, and I think you'll find that they share the qualities of how you "make it about them."

Bloggers, Podcasters, and Other Content Creators

Reaching out to bloggers, podcasters, and other content creators is a key element to a successful crowdfunding campaign. Bloggers are the new press—they're how you organically spread the word about your campaign. There are some key pitfalls you can make when researching and reaching out to bloggers, many of which fall into the "make it about you" category.

In this example, you've created a new iPhone case that vibrates whenever you shout "Hey Siri!" so that you can find it in your house.

Make It about You

You rarely read other blogs or comment on them. The only blog you're interested in is your own. When you do comment on another blog, it is to reference your blog and promote yourself.

Two weeks into your campaign you realize that it's not going well, so you compile a list of blogs that can help promote your product. You send a mass e-mail to all of those blogs. On the mass e-mail, you ask them to promote the crowdfunding campaign as much as possible. A few bloggers write entries about your product, but you don't comment or share those entries.

Make It about Them

Subscribe to a number of blogs, and make a point to comment on at least one of them a day. Only mention your product if it adds to the conversation.

Send personalized e-mails to every blogger you'd like to connect with a month before the campaign begins. Show your respect to them by giving them ample time to plan a post about your project. Demonstrate in each e-mail that you read their blog and appreciate what they do for the iPhone case industry. Mention a few ways that you could add value to their blog's audience. You reference a recent entry on the blog about iPhone case manufacturers, and you mention that you've done a lot of research on those manufacturers that you could share in a guest entry or interview. You don't ask them to promote your project at all—instead, you try to add value to the blogger and his or her audience.

When the blog entries about your project are posted, you share them on Facebook, Twitter, and your project updates. You also comment on them and make yourself available for questions. You realize that this is how you can add value to the bloggers—by letting more people know about their blog.

I've received my fair share of boilerplate e-mails from people asking me to promote their project. I delete them immediately. I've also received e-mails from people who clearly are familiar with my blog and my projects, and even if I can tell they're looking for promotion, they make me feel a little bit important (and some of them even make me laugh). Those e-mails are a breath of fresh air. You want to be a breath of fresh air, not an auto-delete.

This is a huge paradigm shift. A common business practice is to be clear about *your* desires and to aggressively pursue *your* priorities and agendas. The truth is that focusing outward, not inward, will make you a far more successful crowdfunding entrepreneur.

CHAPTER 6

Backers Are Individuals, Not Numbers

A month after I shipped Viticulture, a backer in the Netherlands sent me an e-mail. He was a bulk backer, so he received six full copies of Viticulture for about $30 each, a price point that led to no profit for Stonemaier Games because of all the custom components we crammed into the box (something I wouldn't recommend to other project creators—budget better than I did!).

The backer told me that he had lost his job the day he received the shipment of Viticulture, and he was suddenly faced with the prospect of paying the bills for his family without an income. So he put five of his six copies of Viticulture on eBay. Thanks to the secondary market for the full game at that time, he was able to cover his monthly rent, utilities, and groceries by using the profits from the sales of those five games alone.

He wrote to me to thank me for that unintended utility but also to offer his help. He had read that shipping replacement parts to Europe was expensive, and he volunteered to use his final copy of Viticulture for that purpose. I declined his kind offer, but I was genuinely touched. I didn't know when I made Viticulture that it would affect someone in that way, but I'm so glad it did. The message from the backer was a great reminder to me that crowdfunding campaigns are about the people who make them happen.

Get Your Foot in the Door

Asking for money is *hard.* And because it's hard, we often disguise it in creative ways so that it doesn't feel like we're asking for money. I bet you've received (or sent) at least one mass e-mail in the last year from someone looking to raise money for their 5K relay team in support of a charitable organization. Look at all those layers between you and the money: the mass e-mail, the run, the team, the charity. We go through great lengths to avoid directly asking for money.

You know what? That's okay. The key is that you find a way to do it. The success of your first crowdfunding project hinges on your willingness to ask people for money, particularly friends and family during the first few days of the project.

I spent the first two to three days of the Viticulture campaign sending personal e-mails to everyone I knew. My goal wasn't to get them to give me X amount of money. Rather, my goal was to motivate them to *look at the project page*. As I talked about in the previous chapter, I tried to make each e-mail about the recipient by identifying the aspect of the project I thought he or she would find the most interesting: If the person loved wine, I suggested they check out the project page to see how we incorporated winemaking into a game; if the person was an entrepreneur, I recommended that they look at the project page from a business perspective; and if I knew the person had a great sense of humor or loved movies, I pointed out our outlandish project video.

And so on. I wasn't trying to sell a product; rather, I was trying to connect with someone, perhaps even someone with whom I hadn't spoken in quite some time. In each e-mail, I made sure to let the person know what crowdfunding is. Despite the popularity of the idea, crowdfunding is still a foreign concept to many people.

My personal appeals worked wonders to provide some forward momentum for the campaign. Approximately 10 percent of Viticulture backers ended up being friends and family, many of them contributing in the first few days, when Viticulture raised about $9,000 of its $25,000 goal. That's just about as good as it gets for crowdfunding—if you go with a less personal route, expect to get about 2–5 percent of your financial support from that demographic. Friends and family might help you in other ways (for example, sharing the project link on social media), but actually giving you money is fairly rare.

There is a psychological tool called the "foot in the door" technique that you can use when reaching out to friends and family for support. The idea is that if you show up at someone's house (this is a metaphor—don't actually show up at peoples' homes asking for pledges) and ask them to buy a full kitchen renovation, they're not going to listen to you. It's too big an expense. But if you try to sell them something small instead—perhaps a new microwave—they might consider it. They might even say yes. Then they realize that they need to update the trim around the microwave because it no longer matches the countertops, and the sink is dreadfully outdated. All of a sudden, they have a new kitchen, all because you started small and got your foot in the door.

The $1 pledge is how you get your foot in the door. When you send out personal appeals, ask people to pledge $1, or just to follow the project (backers at any level get project updates e-mailed to them automatically). Of course, make sure you have a $1 reward level to make it easy for people to back you for that amount. It's really not that hard to ask for $1, nor is it hard for someone to give you $1. You'll be surprised at how many of those people end up backing your project at a more significant reward level, and how many share the project on social media.

In a statistical analysis of thousands of Kickstarter projects,[1] John Coveyou found that 44.8 percent of projects with a $1 reward successfully reached their funding goal, compared with 41.7 percent for projects without $1 rewards. The gap triples for projects from first-time creators. Within that group, 39.6 percent who had the $1 reward successfully funded, compared with only 28.8 percent of projects without that reward.

At Stonemaier, we have fun with our $1 pledges—we call it the "backer toast." For every backer who pledges at that level or adds $1 to their pledge, we'll toast them with beer or wine in an uncut video after the campaign ends. As the number of people who request the toast has grown to well over 250 backers, our sips have gotten smaller, but we really enjoy the experience of acknowledging backers one by one on camera.

Here are a few other examples of effective, engaging, and thematic $1 rewards:

- On the Soberdough project ($10,074 raised from 254 backers), a bread mix requiring only beer as the active ingredient, the $1 reward level (limited to five backers) offered a few lucky people the chance to receive a bag of Soberdough mix during the campaign in exchange for a promise to create a written or video review. Those reviewers acted as taste-testers for the rest of the backers.

- On the Lanterns project, a board game about the Chinese harvest festival, if you backed at the $1 reward level, the creators (Foxtrot Games) promised to place an actual floating lantern in water and dedicate it in your honor.

- On the Lift Off! project, a board game set on an exploding planet, the stop-motion video features little alien tokens panicking and avoiding the explosion. In keeping with this theme, Eduardo Baraf offered to save an alien token on video for each backer at the $1 level.

- This was a $5 reward level, but it's still worth mentioning: on the Coolest cooler project (over $13 million in funding from 62,642 backers—that's a lot of doors to get your foot through!), Ryan Grepper offered to write each backer's name on his personal cooler.

The Top Five Ways to Treat Backers As Individuals, Not Numbers

Thanks to my personal appeals to friends and family, Viticulture got off to a fast start, but it still took 19 days to reach its funding goal. It was what I did during the two weeks in between that defined the project. These five methods have been replicated by many other projects on Kickstarter in various categories, and I recommend them to any creator.

Individual Thank-You Messages to Every Backer

The true blessing of crowdfunding is that you know the name of each and every person who pledges to support your product. Compare that to the thousands of products on the shelf at Walmart. If you get Walmart to sell your product, you have no idea who buys it unless that customer goes out of her way to contact you. Crowdfunding makes the transaction personal.

When someone pledges to your crowdfunding project, you get an e-mail telling you that you have a new backer and what his name is. You can click on that message to go to that backer's profile, which shows other projects he's backed, where he's from, and a profile photo.

Whenever I got a new pledge notification for Viticulture, I saved that message in my inbox until I had a minute to spare (I had a full-time day job), and then I composed a personal thank-you note to that backer. I made sure to mention something specific about his profile, and I often asked if he had any questions or feedback as a way to show that I appreciated the backer as an *individual*. Because that's what a backer is in a crowdfunding project—an individual, not some number on a sales report spreadsheet you get from Walmart.

It's difficult to quantify the results, but from the feedback I received, people remembered those personal messages. The thank-you e-mails made Viticulture stand out from other crowdfunding campaigns. It's one thing to get a new backer, but it's quite another to *keep* a backer—every little thing you do helps to establish trust and loyalty.

Also, I made some fantastic contacts thanks to those messages. Several people who responded later became advisory board members, ambassadors, playtesters, or proofreaders. One of them happened to be an editor at the well-read GeekDad blog, which led to a review of Viticulture on the site during the campaign.

Another company that tried this personal approach is Soberdough, which launched its campaign in June 2013. The creators of Soberdough, Veronica and Jordan Hawbaker, added to my personal thank-you model by asking each backer a specific question: "How did you discover our campaign?"

A number of backers responded to that question, creating a wealth of information for Veronica and Jordan that they wouldn't otherwise have had: a large percentage of backers were gamers looking for something easy and delicious to make for game nights. Thanks to that information, Soberdough was able to realign its marketing efforts during the campaign, resulting in the company surpassing its $2,100 funding goal by nearly 500 percent.

If you're thinking, "It will take way too much time to thank each backer," then you really have to consider how much this project means to you. If you're trying to crowdfund your dream project and you can't spend two hours thanking one hundred backers, then maybe it's not really your dream project.

The Money-Back Guarantee

The number one barrier to entry for a backer, especially when considering a project by an unknown crowdfunder, is *trust*. How can you trust that this stranger is going to make something worth your money? How can you trust that she'll follow through on her promises, or at least do her best? How can you trust that she'll communicate with you and be honest with you?

For a backer, it's a leap of faith. I recognized that with Viticulture, and I decided to make it less of a leap and more of a gentle step: we offered a money-back guarantee exclusively to Kickstarter backers of Viticulture.

The terms for our money-back guarantee were as follows: "If you pledge to support Viticulture on Kickstarter and you decide that the game isn't for you within one month of receiving it, you may return it to us for a full refund." The one-month limit was there simply because almost all games will eventually overstay their welcome; this gives backers a reason to play Viticulture right away (multiple times, I hope, before making a final judgment) and then make an informed choice about returning it.

We were establishing trust. In doing so, we eliminated the biggest barrier to entry. Whenever you consider buying something, you're faced with some barriers to entry: cost, time, effort, and image. As the creator-seller, the more barriers I can remove, the better. In this case, I removed the barriers of trust and cost. A backer might look at Viticulture and think, "I might like that, *but* it costs $39, and I might not like it." With a money-back guarantee, there is no "but."

In the long term, a time-sensitive money-back guarantee has the added benefit of inspiring many backers to use the product (in our case, to play the game) as soon as it's released. This is a great way to create buzz if the retail release closely follows delivery to backers.

Of course, at the time, I was afraid that hundreds of backers would return their copies of Viticulture, forcing me to live out the rest of my days in a house made of shame and discarded Viticulture boxes. But that fear translated into accountability—I felt accountable to deliver on my promises.

How did the money-back guarantee turn out? For Viticulture, I shipped 1,300 copies of the game to backers. The total number of money-back requests was ... drumroll ... zero. Yep, zero. No one sent Viticulture back to me. Granted, this doesn't mean that all backers liked Viticulture, but something compelled them not to send it back to me for a refund.

Here are a few reasons that explain this phenomenon:

- **Viticulture is a good-looking game**   My graphic designer and Panda did a great job with the components. We didn't skimp on anything—all pieces are custom and unique, and Beth Sobel's and Jacqui Davis's art in the game looks great. If you make a good-looking product, people are more likely to treasure it *even if they don't use it.*

- **Many people enjoy playing Viticulture**   In some industries this would be anecdotal evidence at best, but in the board-game community, on the website called BoardGameGeek, people rate games on a 1–10 scale. The number one game on BGG as of May 2015 is Twilight Struggle, which has a rating of 8.34. Viticulture has a very solid rating of 7.74.

- **Backers feel loyal to Stonemaier Games**   We treat everyone with respect, we're extremely responsive, we keep everyone updated, and if someone is missing a piece or needs a replacement part, we send them a new piece within days, no questions asked. My perception is that many of our backers genuinely want us to succeed—they feel invested in Stonemaier.

- **Returning the game is a hassle** This isn't by design. In fact, I have Stonemaier "ambassadors" around the world so that a backer in New Guinea doesn't have to ship a game halfway around the world back to us at his expense. Instead, the backer can ship it to Matias in Japan or Helen in Australia, and that ambassador will use the game for spare parts when other backers spill wine on their copy.

- **Even if someone doesn't like the game, it could serve as a nice gift** This applies to any product, especially since there's a story behind every project.

- **The game is worth more than what backers paid for it** This can happen with any project in which a creator offers the product at less than retail price, especially if the game is a limited or premium edition.

Was Viticulture an anomaly? To date, I've shipped more than twenty thousand units to backers (Viticulture, Euphoria, Tuscany, and the Treasure Chest), and only seven backers have returned their rewards for a refund. With results like that, I continue to feel great about that strategy, and I've featured it on all of our projects.

Social Media Stretch Goals

Despite my failed experiment with the Blank Slate Press Kickstarter campaign, I was still fascinated by the impact of social media on a project. For Viticulture, I decided to integrate social media into the stretch goals.

Stretch goals were introduced by Michael Mindes of Tasty

Minstrel Games during his Eminent Domain campaign in 2010. When the campaign reached its funding goal of $20,000 on November 8, Mindes announced that Tasty Minstrel would add additional components to every game if the company continued to raise money. Current backers had a self-serving reason to continue to share the project, and it gave new backers a reason to pledge to the campaign instead of waiting to buy the game later. Also, it shows that the creator has a backer-first mentality: instead of keeping extra funds for itself as profit, the company injected those funds back into the product to make it better for everyone.

Stretch goals have evolved to become a necessity for any project. When I was preparing for Viticulture, I noticed that most projects had stretch goals tied only to the funding amount, which seemed strange to me. A project's success is more than just about funding—it's also closely tied to the number of backers and the extent to which the project is shared on social media. It goes back to the idea of asking friends and family to back a project for $1. I wanted to give people a number of different ways to contribute to the success of the project, so several of Viticulture's stretch goals were unlocked by the number of times people "Liked" the project page.

These goals are kind of like achievements you unlock in a video game or on Foursquare. It feels good to earn *something*. So every time we reached a new stretch goal, all backers felt like they accomplished something together.

The type of stretch goals appropriate for your project will vary widely depending on the category, but universally these goals should be carefully calibrated so that they don't break a project's budget or delay the production schedule. The best way to calculate the feasibility of stretch goals is to use economies of scale. For example, if a board game costs $8 per unit to manufacture based on the minimum print run of 1,500 copies, if you raise enough money to produce 2,000 copies instead, the cost might drop to $7.50 per unit. Thus, you have 50 cents to work with to upgrade a component or add a few new cards.

On Viticulture, we almost reached a stretch goal ($70,000) that would have let us upgrade all cardboard coins in the game to metal coins. This was an extremely ill-advised stretch goal because metal coins add a huge cost to a game. If you have a component that adds a major cost, it's better to add this component to a special reward level, not as a stretch goal that all backers will receive as part of the price of the core product.

Here are the three rules of stretch goals:

- Stretch goals should add real value to your product.

- Stretch goals should not cause you to lose money or delay the project.

- Stretch goals should be given to every backer who receives your product.

An Interview a Day

When I launched Viticulture, I set a goal for myself: I wanted to have an interview, guest post, mention, or review on at least one blog or podcast every day for the duration of the forty-two-day campaign. I've already discussed the importance of media attention; the key here is that I had a *goal*. I had a target. If a day was drawing to a close and Viticulture hadn't been featured anywhere that day, I was accountable to discover and reach out to make sure I didn't miss another day.

I've found those types of goals to be really important for answering the question "What do I do today?" Richard Bliss (Funding the Dream podcast) will tell you to find *one* new backer. Just one. Find a backer today. That's a great goal if things are really slow on your campaign. Or comment on one blog. Or do what I did and try to get one interview, guest post, mention, or review. You can't do everything every day, but you can do *one* specific thing if you hold yourself accountable. Those baby steps really helped me continuously move Viticulture forward.

Involve Backers in the Creative Process

Daniel Pink brilliantly sums up the idea of "pitch" in his book *To Sell Is Human*: "The purpose of a pitch isn't necessarily to move others immediately to adopt your idea. The purpose is to offer something so compelling that it begins a conversation, brings the other person in as a participant, and eventually arrives at an outcome that appeals to both of you."[2]

A crowdfunding project *is* a pitch. You are pitching your creation to the world to see whether the world decides to embrace it. Every element of your project is part of that pitch—the video, the project page text and images, the reward levels, the funding goal, the stretch goals, everything.

But what is the purpose of the pitch? At first glance it would be to compel potential backers to pledge their support, right? I'd like to offer a different perspective that debunks that assumption. This particular insight comes from an example in *To Sell Is Human*.[3]

The boardrooms of Hollywood are where hundreds of agents and screenwriters pitch their films to movie executives every day. Two researchers, Kimberly Elsbach and Roderick Kramer, spent five years observing the pitch process in Hollywood. Day after day they watched people walk into rooms with their dreams on their sleeves, and many walked away with nothing. Sound familiar?

However, over time, as the data accumulated, a clear pattern emerged about the successful pitches: the screenwriters and agents who got the execs to say yes were those who *invited the executives to be collaborators:* "The more the executives—often derided by their supposedly more artistic counterparts as 'suits'—were able to contribute, the better the idea often became, and the more likely it was to be green-lighted." In the context of crowdfunding, the study suggests that the more you're able to make your potential backers feel like collaborators, the more likely they are to back your project.

On many of the most successful projects, the creators are active in the comments, gathering thoughts, opinions, and feedback. Their products are 90–95 percent complete—enough to represent their vision but with some wiggle room for backer collaboration. They have print-and-play files available so that backers can test the games during the project and proofread the rules. They post polls and surveys to name elements of the product. They have reward levels that subtly incorporate people into the product.

Just as with those Hollywood pitches, it's these types of engaging projects that grow to epic proportions. And they're the better for it—all of that feedback results in a richer product. In those cases, crowdfunding is a platform for conversation, collaboration, and mutual creation.

Reaching the Funding Goal

On the morning of September 12, 2012, my phone buzzed with an incoming text. Then another. Then another. Viticulture had funded.

When I went to bed the night before, we were at 85 percent of our funding goal. With weeks to go in the campaign, it was inevitable that we would fund, but I didn't think it would happen for another five to seven days. Then Kickstarter surprised me.

Every day, the Kickstarter staff selects a few projects to feature. They're called "staff picks," and they get prominently featured on Kickstarter's website, thus drawing a lot of attention from window shoppers. To this day I don't know why Kickstarter decided to feature Viticulture, but I'm honored that they did. Viticulture received nearly $7,000 during the twenty-four hours it was featured as a staff pick, driving funding from 85 percent to 110 percent.

My lifelong dream had come true. I cried happy tears, replied to the texts and the jubilant comments on Kickstarter, and went to work at my day job. It was *really* hard to focus that day. When I got home, I filmed a short video announcement on my iPad for that night's update so that people could see on my face how much their pledges meant to me. I still get a little teary eyed watching myself say, "I found out this morning, as many of you probably did as well, that ... we're making a board game!"

As creators, we have the opportunity to look out into the crowd and see individual people, not a ubiquitous mass. That's why each of the people on the cover of this book is unique and colorful and not a blurry gray figure.

CHAPTER 7

How to Make Friends and Lose Money

I love spreadsheets. I love sorting and summarizing data. I love creating budgets and projections. I love plugging in various numbers to see how they impact the bottom line.

Despite my meticulous use of spreadsheets to figure out the costs for Viticulture, I made a mistake in calculating international shipping costs. Instead of treating each backer as an individual and charging shipping fees based on a backer's specific location, I lumped all overseas backers into the same category, charging each of them $20 for shipping. I had seen other projects do this, so I thought it would be fine. I had built into the pledge level about $10 for shipping (therefore offering "free" shipping to US backers), so shipping for international backers was essentially $30. I figured that would be more than enough for locations like Canada and a little less than needed for Australia, South America, Asia, and the EU. It would balance out—no problem.

In December of 2012, I realized this was actually a *big* problem. The project had successfully funded to the tune of $65,980 from 942 backers. Seventy-one percent of them were from the United States and 5 percent were from Canada—games headed to those backers weren't an issue. The issue was the remaining 24 percent (226 backers). For those backers, the minimum shipping cost using the US Postal Service was $45, and it went up to $55 for places like Australia, Japan, and Brazil. After placing the order with Panda Game Manufacturing, I barely had enough cash on hand to fulfill orders based on the original $20 fee. I didn't have the additional

$4,520 I'd need to fulfill international orders. Was Stonemaier Games doomed to fail before we delivered our first game?

Creators Eat Last

Simon Sinek's second book, *Leaders Eat Last,* is about how organizations that make their employees feel safe are more successful. As Sinek summarizes in his TEDTalk on the subject: "When a leader makes the choice to put the safety and lives of the people inside the organization first, to sacrifice their comforts and sacrifice the tangible result so the people feel safe and feel like they belong, remarkable things happen."[1]

Great project creators—great *leaders*—make their backers feel safe. They consistently show their backers that they're in good hands by putting the needs of the backers before their own. In return, as Sinek says, remarkable things happen.

Sinek uses the example of officers in the US Marines in one of his TEDTalks. The Marine custom is that officers eat last, which sometimes means that there's no food left for them. This happened in the particular story Sinek tells, but then Marines started bringing an officer portions of their food to share. They sacrificed for him because they knew that he would sacrifice for them.

The same thing can happen to crowdfunders who put the needs of the backers before their own. For example, it is highly likely that something will cost more than you originally budgeted. You will have a choice: remove or diminish the item in question, ask backers for more money, or dig into your own pockets to make the thing as awesome as you first envisioned—or, even better, make it *more* awesome. If you do this, backers will see the type of leader you are, and they will follow you.

It's about more than the money. It's the time and effort you spend trying to deliver by the estimated delivery date. It's how you communicate with backers with complete honesty and transparency. When backers see that you're willing to share good news *and* bad news, they know that you're not hiding anything from them, and they will trust you.

You can't tell people "trust me" and expect them to trust you. You have to earn that trust time after time through your actions. When people trust you to share their ideas and creativity during and after a crowdfunding campaign, remarkable things can happen. If you foster a community-driven environment where you listen to people and respect their ideas—an environment where people feel *safe* to offer their opinions—you will see your project blossom into something far beyond your wildest dreams.

The Early Bird Catches Few Worms

One of the most contentious elements of crowdfunding campaigns is the concept of *early-bird rewards*. I featured an early-bird reward level on the Viticulture campaign because my research showed that a lot of other campaigns had early birds. (This is a common mistake—just because other campaigns do something doesn't make it right). At the time I didn't think about the long-term repercussions of the early-bird pledge level and how it could be bad for the majority of backers.

An early-bird reward is almost always a discounted price for a limited number of products. Viticulture's early-bird pledge level was limited to one hundred people for a copy of the game at $35 (compared with $39 for all other backers).

I can now say with confidence that including an early-bird reward level on Viticulture was a mistake, and I can prove it.

Forward momentum is incredibly important when you're

running a crowdfunding campaign, particularly in the first few days. However, I think many project creators (myself included for Viticulture) assume that early-bird pledge levels are the best way to get the project off the ground at the beginning.

Let's be clear about that: the sole purpose of early-bird pledge levels is to give potential backers a reason to pledge now—on the first few days of a creator's first crowdfunding project—instead of later.

However, the true impact of early-bird rewards is that the lucky few backers who happen to discover the project early on get a discount, and everyone else—the potentially thousands of backers who follow—are charged more, even though all backers are pledging for the project to exist. My philosophy is that the entire campaign should be treated like one big early bird, given that *all* backers are pledging their hard-earned money for something that they won't even receive for six to twelve months.

That said, I understand the temptation of offering an early-bird reward level. You want to give the project a little boost at the beginning, right? Here are some of the damaging effects and downsides to consider:

- **You create winners and losers**   On your crowdfunding project, you want all backers to feel like winners. You do that by making something awesome, offering reasonably priced pledge levels, and running an engaging campaign. You don't want any backers to feel like they "lost." But that's exactly what early-bird pledge levels do. One hundred people might "win" the better price, but you've created a situation in which everyone else feels like they lost. It might just be a little twinge—"Aw shucks, I wish I had known about the project on the first day"—but you don't want any backer to feel that way. Some backers are so turned off even by the idea that you have an early-bird level that they won't back your project (that's a bit extreme, but it's fairly common).

- **You create confusion later in the project**   Say you have a $25 early-bird level for your gourmet marshmallow project, with a standard reward level price of $30. Two weeks into the project, based on backer feedback, you add a pledge level for $35 that upgrades the standard marshmallows to chocolate-dipped marshmallows ... but you know that you can make only one hundred of those marshmallows based on the production process. It's easy to add a new reward level limited to one hundred people, and just as easy for your standard-level backers to upgrade to that level. But what about the early-bird backers? They're the ones who were there from the beginning—they formed the foundation of your project. Now you're telling them that the only way they can get the special chocolate-dipped marshmallows is to spend what everyone else has to spend? You can't simply let them add on $5 because of your production limitations. So now even the early-bird backers feel like they lost. This example provides just a tiny taste of the conundrums you create by starting out with an early-bird pledge level.

- **Cancellations are extremely visible**   Even the best project in the world will have cancellations. Imagine how people's impressions of your project would change over time if all backers got an e-mail notification every time someone cancelled. Not good, right? Well, in a way that's what early-bird cancellations do. It's quite visible when someone cancels from an early-bird level, and it doesn't inspire confidence in your existing backers. It's also not good for new backers. Have you ever stumbled on a project on day 20 and seen a few unfilled early-bird slots? It suddenly makes you wonder if there's something wrong with the project that you overlooked the first time.

- **You dilute your brand when you open up more early-bird pledge levels**   I'll admit it—I once grabbed the last early-bird reward level for a Kickstarter project, and it felt good. Yay for me saving $8. I felt like one of the "winners" I described earlier. Then, two days later, I got an update from the project creator saying that due to the "unexpected success" of the early-bird level, he was going to add a new early-bird level, splitting the difference between the original level and the standard level. I've even seen project creators do this at the same price. When creators use gimmicks like this, they lose the trust of backers.

Without early-bird rewards, how can you get backers during the first few days of your project, when momentum is incredibly important? Here are some ways that are better for backers than early-bird rewards:

- **Build a community in advance**   This goes back to those steps you can take to build a community of people who share your passion before launching your project. Not only are these your most eager customers on launch day, but if you've tried to connect with these people in an outward-facing way leading up to the project, they're the ones who will be most excited to support *you*.

- **Have a great product on a great project page**   Do you know what's more compelling than a gimmick like an early-bird level for getting backer support? Create a great product and a great project page. If you make something that people get excited about from day 1, they're not going to hit the Remind

Me button. They're going to back it right away so that they won't miss out on something amazing.

- **Offer a fair price**   If your budget allows you to offer one hundred people the product at $45 instead of $50, I bet you could make the lower price available to all backers.

- **Offer a timed stretch goal for everyone**   Instead of offering a perk just for the first few backers, create a time-sensitive stretch goal that benefits all backers. The tabletop game project Trickerion did this brilliantly in January 2015. If this project reached its funding goal of $30,000 within the first week of the campaign, the creators would double the number of unique role cards in the game. With backers working together to spread the word about the project, the project met its goal in less than twenty-four hours.

- **Offer creative, compelling limited reward levels**   Give backers a chance to be a part of your product or get an extra special version of it. Early-bird reward levels don't increase engagement, involvement, or loyalty, but other limited reward levels do.

- **Appeal to friends and family**   To a first-time project creator, friends and family can be an incredible asset over the first few days. Spend that time writing individual e-mails to everyone you know to help jump-start your campaign.

Regardless of my personal philosophy about early-bird rewards, it really comes down to what backers think. As of April 2015, here are the results (shown in fig. 4) of a long-running poll on my blog.

Of the backers who have a preference, more than 65 percent are turned off by early-bird rewards. Your chances of crowdfunding success are significantly higher if you put backers first by not offering an early-bird pledge level.

As a backer, how do you feel about early-bird reward levels?

Answer	Votes	Percent	
I don't like them	155	50%	
I like them!	82	27%	
I'm ambivalent	72	23%	

FIGURE 4. Poll results showed that half of the backers who responded didn't like early-bird rewards.

The White Whale of Worldwide Shipping

There is one caveat to transparent communication: it doesn't mean much if you're not solution focused. An update in which you outline all the problems your project is having needs to conclude with a clear plan for how you're going to fix the problem.

Back in December 2012, I didn't have a solution for my shipping problem. At least I had identified the issue well in advance of order fulfillment, so I had several months to figure it out.

I'm far from the first creator to face a shipping issue. Some have asked backers for additional funds, but that never occurred to me (it seems like a quick way to lose trust). Others have issued refunds to backers in certain locations. And countless others have incurred a significant loss when shipping worldwide.

When I got to the heart of the problem, though, it wasn't about the money. I could exhaust my personal savings if needed. The problem was that there wasn't a good solution in place for delivering crowdfunding rewards to backers, regardless of their location. At the time, most creators were still rolling up their sleeves and hand packing every reward. In fact, I had already sent out some Viticulture rewards (wine glasses and corkscrews) by hand. It was inefficient, time-consuming, full of risk (what if your garage is attacked by ninja koalas?), and expensive. There had to be a better way.

I started looking into fulfillment companies that could handle the packing and shipping for me. There are plenty of these companies, but the more I read about Amazon's multichannel fulfillment, the more I knew it was a good fit. I could send pallets of games to an Amazon warehouse in the United States, upload a spreadsheet of addresses, and Amazon (a company built around efficient shipping) would send the games to backers quickly and at a low cost. In fact, the cost was lower than if I shipped the packages myself because Amazon buys cardboard boxes by the tens of millions and has great discounts with all major couriers in the United States.

But the United States wasn't the problem. My concern was the group of 265 international backers. Amazon in the United States doesn't offer overseas multichannel fulfillment services for most products, only media items like books and CDs. This is when I learned the value of talking to people outside my usual sphere of influence to get some new perspectives. It increases your chances of getting lucky.

While at a staff Christmas party for my day job in mid-December 2012, I found myself talking to the president of my organization's advancement council, Greg Sonnenberg. Greg happened to be a Viticulture backer, so he asked how the project was coming along, and I said that production was going well but I was a little worried about shipping.

As Greg listened, I described how expensive it was to ship products internationally from the United States. I explained my solution for US backers and how I wished I could do the same thing for backers worldwide. "Well, why can't you?" Greg said. "Amazon has fulfillment centers all over the world. Just ship a pallet of games to each of them."

My first reaction was to come up with excuses for why it wouldn't work. Greg's solution was daunting—how could I possibly coordinate freight shipping to places like Canada and Germany?

But the more Greg outlined the idea, the more I started to think it was the key to worldwide fulfillment. When I got home that night, I looked into other Amazon fulfillment centers. Sure enough, there were several in Canada and the EU. Each offered the same low prices for shipping within the country or region. Both were considerably more cost effective and efficient than shipping by hand from the United States.

The best benefit of all wouldn't emerge until months later: when shipping games to backers from *within* their own country (or the EU) instead of sending them one by one from the United States, the backers didn't have to pay value-added tax (VAT) or customs fees. By finding a better shipping solution for Stonemaier Games, I had stumbled on a way to relieve a huge burden from backers.

As I write this, I've used Amazon multichannel fulfillment on Viticulture, Euphoria, Tuscany, and the Treasure Chest to great success. I have seller accounts set up at Amazon.com, Amazon.ca, Amazon.de, and Amazon.co.uk. Meanwhile, I've also forged relationships with other shipping companies, such as Ideaspatcher in France, Good Games in Australia, and Agility in China. By finding better ways to ship, I've been able to lower shipping costs to Kickstarter backers across the board, and I've seen the percentage of international backers on our projects grow from 29 percent on Viticulture to 39 percent on Euphoria and 42 percent on Tuscany. Tens of thousands of people have read a blog entry I wrote that outlined the step-by-step procedures for using Amazon fulfillment. In the meantime, other fulfillment services have realized the market potential for Kickstarter reward fulfillment and have specifically reached out to project creators to offer their services.

These fulfillment services are for crowdfunding projects both big and small. It's worth finding and budgeting for solutions like these in advance. (Don't wait until after the project like I did!) You might send only three cartons of products to Ideaspatcher in France for EU fulfillment, but for most products that's still much more cost effective—for you and for your backers—than to ship those products individually from the United States. By offering optimized shipping options during the project, you significantly increase your chances of attracting international backers.

Figuring out the "Stonemaier Method" of shipping worldwide will take time and effort, but if you read through my blog posts on the subject,[2] you should be able to figure it out.

Here are my top ten things to keep in mind when planning for order fulfillment. These are all based on mistakes I made that I hope you can avoid.

Top Ten Ways to Prepare Your Product for Worldwide Fulfillment

1. **Figure out shipping before the project launches**   Have a shipping plan for two scenarios: if you barely fund and if you wildly overfund. Get estimates from fulfillment centers and couriers and build them into your budget. Your funding goal should include shipping fees, but you don't know where backers will come from, so estimate using the following breakdown (numbers will vary depending on the type of project): 60 percent United States, 15 percent Western Europe, 10 percent Canada, 5 percent Central Europe, 5 percent Asia, 3 percent Australia/New Zealand, and 2 percent rest of world.

2. **One size doesn't fit all**   Every country is different, so treat them as such. Don't charge $20 for all international backers because you're overcharging for some areas and undercharging for others—that's not fair to your backers or your budget.

3. **Build a shipping subsidy into every pledge**   Backers in the United States have come to expect "free" shipping, which

really means that a shipping subsidy is built into the pledge price. Remember to deduct that subsidy when you are calculating shipping fees for other countries. For example, if the reward price is $30 and $10 of that is shipping, instead of charging the full $15 for shipping to France, charge $5.

4. **Make it EU friendly**   Find a fulfillment company in Europe that will also serve as an importer of record so that you can ship rewards to backers from within Europe, saving backers the cost of high customs, tax, and brokerage fees. The shipping cost to be charged to the backer is the sum of ocean freight per unit, 20 percent VAT per unit (paid on the manufacturing cost of the product), and the shipping fee per unit (this will vary widely throughout Europe, especially between Western and Central Europe).

5. **Don't ship to backers in November or December**   Shipping to backers in November and December is a bad idea because it's the season when everything goes wrong. Ports get backed up. Workers at fulfillment centers barely pad packages because they're trying to get them out the door as soon as possible. Couriers toss boxes from their truck instead of placing them on your front door. Theft goes up. People travel and aren't at their regular address. It's simply not worth the trouble.

6. **Offer bundled deals for international backers**   Everyone likes a good deal on bundled items (like one box of custom soap for $20 or two boxes for $35), but these rewards are particularly appealing to international backers because they can divide the shipping cost among friends. Often this encourages backers to share the project online as they try to find others in their area who are interested in going in on the bundled reward. Make sure to limit the number of units based on the

crowdfunding platform's guidelines (Kickstarter has a ten-unit limit), and scale up the shipping if the units will ship in more than one carton.

7. **Design proper packaging**   Many fulfillment centers and retailers require the product to have unique SKU (stock keeping unit) and bar codes on the outside of the box. Each additional SKU that the fulfillment center has to pack will usually increase the cost (Amazon calls this a "pick-and-pack fee"), so if you can, consolidate multiple items into one container. This includes items that backers add on to their pledge—keep these to a minimum. Also make sure to label the box with the country of origin, as customs might reject the shipment if it doesn't have "Made in China" (or the appropriate country) on it.

8. **Ship directly from the manufacturer to fulfillment centers** Request backer surveys early so that you know exactly how many rewards to send to each region, and add in a 10–20 percent buffer per product to account for damaged or missing rewards. Regardless of where you manufacture your product, arrange with your freight shipping company (I work with Dimerco) to ship directly from the manufacturer to various fulfillment centers around the world. I made the mistake on Viticulture of sending the US and Canada rewards to the United States first, then splitting off the Canadian portion, requiring me to pay customs fees twice instead of once. If you ship any type of wooden product to Australia, you must have a fumigation certificate (they are very strict about this).

9. **Have a distribution plan**   Backer reward fulfillment is your top priority, but if you're trying to make a lasting business out of a successful crowdfunding campaign, you'll need to

sell your product through other venues (distributors, retailers, conventions, e-commerce, and so on). Have a plan for where the extra copies of the product should go well before they leave the manufacturer. Determine the manufacturer's suggested retail price (MSRP) based on your industry; for board games, this means five times the manufacturing cost, and distributors will get a 60 percent discount. For example, a game that costs $8 to make should have an MRSP of $40, and distributors will buy it from you for $16.

10. **Give the fulfillment center specific packing instructions** Your backers' first impression of the reward they've been waiting on for six months will be when they open the shipping package, so you want them to have a great experience. Vet your fulfillment centers in advance to ensure that they know how to pack your particular product. For Amazon multichannel fulfillment, special packaging instructions must be made when you originally schedule the freight shipment (long before the game even leaves the manufacturer).

Stand and Deliver on Schedule

In 2012, CNN reached out to the top fifty most-funded projects on Kickstarter to see how their actual delivery date correlated with their estimated delivery date.[3] The data revealed that only 16 percent of projects delivered on time. The other 84 percent ranged from "a little late" to "really, really late."

Now, before I talk about this, I want to be very clear about something: The words "on time" and "late" are pretty misleading in the context of crowdfunding. All reward levels clearly say "estimated delivery: (month/year)." It's an estimate, not a hard and fast date. Can something be "late" based on an estimate? That's for you to decide.

Is It Important to Deliver by the Estimated Delivery Date?

Yes and no. Yes, you should do everything in your power to deliver your product within the estimated month. It's good for you as the creator to stick to that schedule because it builds confidence and trust. It's good for backers because, well, they get the product they pledged to receive in a timely manner.

However, you should not rush the delivery if the product isn't ready. Backers would much rather have a great, tested, finished product than something that's produced through a rush job and is barely usable.

Figure 5 shows a poll from my blog (results as of April 2015) that shows how backers feel about late projects.

What's your tipping point as a backer for getting frustrated about a delayed project delivery (even if communication from the creator is great)?

Answer	Votes	Percent	
6 months late	54	44%	
3 months late	41	33%	
12 months late	22	18%	
1 month late	6	5%	

FIGURE 5. Many backers begin to feel restless if a project is more than three months late.

Every backer has a tipping point, but the majority seem to start being aggravated when they haven't received their rewards between three to six months after the estimated delivery month.

Is It Even Possible to Deliver by the Estimated Delivery Date?

It's rare but possible. Viticulture and Euphoria delivered early to many backers, on time to most backers, and a few weeks late to a small number of backers in the UK because of a mislabeled pallet.

Most large board-game companies don't even release delivery dates until the games are actually on the boat from the manufacturer (or very close to it). Why is that? Because it's really, really hard to correctly estimate dates many months in advance, even for major publishers who have way more experience than you or me. Crowdfunders don't have the luxury of waiting until the product is on the boat to launch their crowdfunding campaign. Thus the difficulty in delivering on time isn't so much your physical ability to finish the product and deliver it as it is your ability to correctly estimate the delivery schedule.

The best thing you can do to increase your chance of delivering on time is to under promise and over deliver. Estimate your delivery date, and then add two months to it. Continue to operate as though you promised to deliver during the actual estimated month, and if you pull it off, awesome. But having some buffer room to account for all the things that can go wrong when developing a project can be huge.

Don't even attempt to deliver a project in November or December. There's simply too much happening at that time in terms of retailers, shipping companies (freight and courier), and the complications of backers going on vacation (which you will also encounter in August, particularly with European backers). It's great to get products on shelves for the holiday season (after delivering to backers), but if you want that, you should eye October as the very latest delivery month.

Remember that there is no better way to lose future backers than by delivering your product to retailers before you deliver it to backers. Don't do it. If you're working with other parties who have control of when your product is released to retailers (like a distribution broker), make sure you have a very clear, written understanding that the distributor cannot release the game to retailers until you authorize it.

If You're Going to Be Late, Communicate

Good communication will make backers care a lot less that your project is late. They just want to know that you're doing something and that the project is moving forward in some way.

A great example of this is the game Xia: Legends of a Drift System by Cody Miller of Far Off Games ($346,772 raised from 3,293 backers).[4] Xia was originally scheduled to deliver in December 2013, but during the project some stretch goals were added that bumped the date forward to March 2014. The game eventually delivered to backers in October 2014. But Cody did a fantastic job of keeping backers updated every step of the way with sneak peeks behind the scenes about the development and manufacturing process (with lots of photos). That's key. Give backers something interesting to read while they wait for the project, and it won't really feel late anymore.

Take Studio Neat, the company behind five successful crowd-funding campaigns that in total have generated nearly $500,000 in funding. Here's what Dan Provost has to say about issues and communication:

> We have faced two major manufacturing delays, one with the Cosmonaut and one with the Neat Ice Kit. For the Cosmo-naut, we severely underestimated how long it would take to manufacture, so we were constantly having to post updates to our backers about the delay, which was no fun. I feel we have done a much better job with the Neat Ice Kit. Even though there has been a delay, which is never fun, we took it as an opportunity to explain how these delays can happen, and how it's a natural part of the transition to full-scale production. Hopefully, the backers were able to learn something new. The backers have responded very positively, and have been tremendously supportive. We are very grateful!

Dan outlines an important distinction here. When the Cosmonaut was delayed, they kept backers informed through frequent updates, but they didn't involve backers in the process. So, for the Neat Ice Kit, they used delays as an opportunity to teach backers about the behind-the-scenes process of manufacturing something new. They added value to backers—they made it about them.

Brad Martin at Tactical Keychains, creator of eight successfully funded Kickstarter campaigns (including TKMB: Precision Machined, which raised $42,403 from 678 backers), offers similar insights about what he shares with backers: "I tell them everything, I leave nothing out. They love that! I have many 'bad' updates, there is always something going wrong, and instead of hiding it I tell them." Brad uses transparent communication to establish and maintain trust, and that trust has translated into repeat customers on multiple projects.

The one connection that binds creators like Dan and Brad is that they put backers' needs before their own. Instead of asking "How can I make myself look good?" they ask "How can I make backers feel good about their pledge?" They have the backer-first mentality that defines crowdfunding leaders.

During the Euphoria fulfillment month of December 2013, I took communication to the extreme. I was driving home to Virginia from St. Louis for the holidays at the same time that thousands of backers were waiting to get their games before Christmas. The prospect of spending thirteen hours on the road away from my e-mail was disconcerting to me, not because I thought anything major would go wrong, but because I wanted to respond to backers quickly if they had questions or concerns. Taking a cue from Simon Sinek, I wanted them to feel *safe*.

So I sent my personal cell phone number to 4,765 backers. I told backers on a public project update that I was going to be on the road for thirteen hours, and if they had any questions or concerns, they could call me. Only two backers took me up on the offer, both just to say hi. I think they were curious to see whether it was my real phone number.

After backing myself into a corner with the Viticulture shipping issues, I forced myself to find a solution so that I could ship the game to backers on schedule and on budget. I learned that problems can make you a better leader if you talk about them openly with backers and focus on solutions instead of making excuses. In the end, it all comes down to the people for whom you're solving problems. Are you solving problems to help yourself? Or, when something bad happens, do you ask, "How can I fix this for my backers?" When you put backers first, amazing things can happen.

The Perils of Exclusive Content

Something happened after the Euphoria campaign that forced me to make a tough choice between a promise I made to backers and—at least as I perceived it at the time—the future success of my company.

By all accounts, Euphoria was a very successful crowdfunding project. It raised $309,446 from 4,764 very engaged, passionate backers.

One of the key features of the Euphoria campaign was the Kickstarter-exclusive components (fig. 6). Exclusive content is something that a creator includes in some or all of the project rewards, committing to provide that exclusive content only to the project's backers. This isn't a legally binding agreement, but it is a social contract that can retain or lose the trust of backers based on whether the creator keeps her promise. Exclusive components and products are a very common way for creators to entice backers to support the project *now* instead of waiting for *later*, similar to early-bird rewards.

FIGURE 6. The premium resource tokens in Euphoria: clay, gold, and stone are among other tokens from the game.

On the surface, exclusive content fits with my core philosophy of putting backers first and making the project about them. They're putting their money at risk on something that doesn't exist, so it makes sense that they would be rewarded with something no one else can get.

Good idea in principle, bad idea in reality.

So on Euphoria, I offered three very special exclusive components that sent backers into a feeding frenzy at the end of the campaign (the project raised over $85,000 in the final forty-eight hours). The lesser of the three were wooden stars (instead of cardboard stars in the retail version) and a grayscale, double-sided game board (in line with the dystopian theme of the game). The big one was a set of "realistic" resources: gold, stone, and clay tokens that looked and felt like the real thing.

Fast forward six months, when backers around the world are showing off their beautiful resource tokens at game nights, meet-ups, and conventions. Meanwhile, retailers were trying to sell the 3,300 retail versions of the game we had produced, each of which featured wooden resource tokens (they're nice, but they're nowhere close to the realistic versions). I started to get e-mails from nonbackers asking whether they could purchase the game with those components, or at least add the realistic resources to their retail games. Every time I replied the same way: "Sorry, but those resources are exclusive to Kickstarter backers."

Each of these e-mails was bittersweet to write. On one hand, I was upholding the promise I made to my backers—backers who enabled me to make a career from my passion. On the other, it didn't feel right to exclude people. I want to be someone who *includes* people, not *excludes* them.

Also, it was hurting business. Many of the people who wrote to me requesting the resources were very blunt about the fact that without the resources, they would never buy the game. Granted, that's their decision, and they didn't seem like the most pleasant of people to have as customers, but I needed to sell those retail games.

So on January 23, 2014, I wrote a Euphoria project update that would have a significant impact on my perspective on exclusive content. It would ultimately reshape Stonemaier Games into what it is today. I've truncated it here a bit from the original post:

> As I hope you all have seen by everything we do at Stonemaier and that I personally do in all of my interactions with you, we put backers first. I've built Stonemaier on that premise, and I hope to continue to build it with Kickstarter backers in mind. It starts with the Kickstarter campaign and culminates in delivering something to you that you will treasure from the minute you open the box to the tenth time it hits the table.

I would like to ask for your blessing to make the exclusive resources from Euphoria available as a premium add-on directly from Stonemaier Games in the future, both on and off of Kickstarter.

Here's your chance to impact the future of Stonemaier Games with your vote.

I was a bit naïve when I wrote this update. Up until that point, the response of backers to pretty much everything I did for Euphoria was nothing but positive and supportive. However, I saw a new side to some of the backers in the 210 comments that flooded the update over the next few days. The vast majority were actually quite positive and supportive, which should have been encouraging to me. Those backers seemed to fully embrace the philosophy of "inclusion" I was moving toward—instead of hoarding their beautiful resources, they wanted to share them with the world.

But as you will learn on Kickstarter and other crowdfunding sites, the vocal minority is, well, *vocal*. In this case, the vocal minority was furious that I would even suggest the idea to them. They felt like the idea was a betrayal of their trust. They wanted the exclusive components to exist for them and for no one else. I also had the results of a poll to consider (fig. 7).

What do you think about Stonemaier offering the special Euphoria resources at a premium price outside of Kickstarter?

Answer	Votes	Percent	
I'm fine with it	1,107	90%	
I'm against it	123	10%	

Total votes = 1,230

FIGURE 7. The results of this poll showed that most backers supported my goal of producing exclusive content in the future.

Again, the survey results were extremely encouraging in regard to the majority of backers sharing my philosophy of inclusion. But I couldn't ignore the 10 percent who were flat-out against the idea. I didn't agree with the minority, but they were backers like everyone else, and it was important for me to respect them.

After much contemplation and discussions with a few advisors and my business partner, I decided to not produce more of the special components featured in the original version of Euphoria. Instead, Stonemaier Games would produce a new line of premium game accessories, and we would swear off exclusive content forever.

This was a pivotal moment for me and Stonemaier Games. As difficult as those two days were, I felt a huge burden lift off my back. No longer was I bound by chains to the rock that is exclusive content. I was free to make something new—perhaps even something better—for everyone. I was free to offer our future content in an inclusive, welcoming way to backers and future customers alike. While exclusives might help a single campaign and create a fun experience for the backers, if you're trying to build a company and a lasting brand from that campaign, they end up doing more harm than good. They alienate anyone who discovers the product after that very slim window of the crowdfunding campaign.

A few months after the Euphoria discussion, how did Tuscany do without any exclusive content? It raised $450,333 from 4,333 backers who were 100 percent on board with the philosophy of inclusion. *Hell yeah.*

Over the next few months, I frequently discussed on my blog and on the Funding the Dream podcast the idea of getting rid of exclusive content. There aren't many philosophies that I so fervently endorse, but I had personally experienced the negative effects of exclusives firsthand and wanted to save other creators the trouble.

To those creators, I present the following. These are ranked in descending order based on a poll on my blog:

Ten Better Reasons to Compel Backers to
Support Your Project Than Exclusive Rewards

1. **Improve the product via stretch goals**   With stretch goals, every bit of funding makes the product better for *everyone*, including you.

2. **Discounted price**   A project should offer a lower price for the product than retail MSRP.

3. **Promo content included now for free, later at a price**
   There are ways to get content that feels exclusive without it being truly limited to backers. Sometimes it's in the form of promo cards that a creator offers only during the project, at conventions, and through special promotions. Other times it's in the form of alternative art. Or if you want to go big, creators can separate many of the stretch-goal components (which are included in the project rewards) into a separate "enhancement pack" to sell by itself after the campaign. You're getting something for the same set price now that others will have to buy separately in the future—but at least they have the chance to get it.

4. **Belief in creator**   This project is your dream—not just to create something for you, but to create something for them—to create something that backers will cherish and treasure for a long time. If backers believe in what they're doing, the crowdfunding project is the time and the place for them to share their passion by supporting you.

5. **Funding need**   A project needs backer funds even if it has already reached its funding goal—every little bit really does help. Those extra dollars are going toward making the product and getting it to backers, not toward rum and Ferraris.

6. **Receive it before retailers**   Deliver the product to backers well before it's released to retailers and distributors.

7. **Limited supply**   Just because something isn't exclusive doesn't mean it's not limited. Publishers and other creators can't make infinite numbers of things—everything is finite. So if a backer wants the product, now might be the only time to get it.

8. **Influence the final product**   Offer polls and discussions that allow backers to shape the future of the product.

9. **Engage with the community**   Sure, if you back a lot of projects, you don't have time to be an active member of every project community. But from my experience, every now and then a project comes along that I really want to talk about with people who are just as excited about it as I am, and the time I spend on those comment threads is worth every second.

10. **Optimized shipping and customs**   By supporting the project from its inception, backers create an opportunity for shipping optimization. When I decide how many pallets of my games I send to Canada, Australia, Asia, France, the UK, or Germany for fulfillment within those countries or regions, I base that number on the formula (# of backer games + # of extra games in case the backer games get damaged or stolen). Thus, nonbackers often end up spending significantly more on shipping fees and customs to get the game from the United States.

By focusing on these elements instead of on the fear-of-missing-out tactic of exclusive content, you will build a much stronger community . . . and a lasting company.

When You Go Above and Beyond, Your Backers Will Rally around You

A few months after my Tuscany Kickstarter campaign, something happened that shows how special things can happen as a result of good communication and the willingness to put backers first.

Earlier in the chapter I discussed the importance—and the challenge—of delivering as close to the estimated delivery date as possible. Despite my detailed scheduling and planning, however, I realized in October 2014 that Tuscany wasn't going to ship to backers in November as planned. In hindsight, I shouldn't have estimated November as the shipping date at all for such a complex game—January would have been better.

Normally this wouldn't drive me to do anything extreme, but I really wanted to deliver to backers before the December holiday season. So I talked to my shipping company and decided to send all backer copies of Tuscany to Canada and Europe via air freight at an additional cost of $24,000 (normally a made-in-China product like this would be shipped via slower, cheaper ocean freight). Asia and Australia weren't a concern because of their proximity to our manufacturer in China, and the huge US shipment would go out first in the hopes of making it to the United States by December.

I announced the plan to the Tuscany backers, bracing myself for the prospect of people groaning about yet another crowdfunding project delivering after the estimated delivery date. But the 100+ comments on the post were the exact opposite. Not only were people completely understanding, a number of backers in Canada and Europe said that they would be happy to wait until January for the slower ocean freight shipment.

So rather than make a blanket decision for all backers in those areas, I created an online form for any Canadian or European backer to fill out if he or she wanted to be a part of the more expensive air freight delivery. The results were incredible: before I offered the option, 1,823 copies of Tuscany were to be air freighted. After the option was offered, only 495 copies of Tuscany had to be shipped via air freight.

As a result of my backers' flexibility, I had to spend only $6,500 extra instead of $24,000. It goes to show that if you put your backers first, good things happen.

To repeat the words of Simon Sinek: "When a leader makes the choice to put the safety and lives of the people inside the organization first, to sacrifice their comforts and sacrifice the tangible result so the people feel safe and feel like they belong, remarkable things happen."

By trying my best to put backers first every step of the way—to make them feel safe, respected, and included—I earned their trust, and I learned a lot about being a leader. I believe that those short-term losses translate into long-term success for a crowdfunded company like Stonemaier Games.

CHAPTER 8

Go Small to Win Big

There is one counterintuitive concept that every crowdfunder should embrace: if you want your project to be a *big* success, make almost every aspect of it as *small* as possible. This goes against much of what we've been taught about startups. The new companies that get the most media attention are those with big-name investors and big, expensive product launches. We're told that more is better—more options, more customization, more Facebook Likes, more re-tweets. We hear that size matters, whether it's the length of the movie or the number of pages in the new *Game of Thrones* novel. The bigger, the better.

But with crowdfunding, the opposite is true. Focused, personal campaigns are better for backers, and thus result in greater short- and long-term results for creators.

The Value of One Backer

A 2014 study published by behavioral psychologist Dr. Arnout van de Rijt[1] showed that early support of a project translates into more funding from other sources than projects without early support.

Dr. van de Rijt picked 200 new and unfunded Kickstarter projects at random. He chose half of them (also at random) and contributed either 1 percent or 10 percent of their funding goal.

Of the projects in the control group—those to which van de Rijt did not pledge—only 39 percent of projects in the control group received even a single other pledge during the twenty-four-day trial period. However, of the projects that received contributions from van de Rijt, 70 percent received at least one other donation.

That's a significant difference. Basically, the study shows that people are more likely to join the party if they're not the first ones on the dance floor.

The study goes on to show, remarkably, that the size of the pledge didn't affect that 70 percent number at all. It's not a matter of size or quantity—it's the mere presence of a backer that makes a project more compelling to other potential backers. The nice thing about this is that your job just got a lot easier. All you have to do is get *one* backer and your chances of getting subsequent backers jumps from 39 percent to 70 percent. Every time you're struggling to figure out what to do next on your campaign, just try to get one more backer. Just one. You can do that!

Lowest Possible Funding Goal

Project creators need to make their backers believe that *a project has a chance at funding*. If a backer discovers your project page and sees a $100,000 funding goal, that's a daunting number. They might doubt (justifiably so) the likelihood of you reaching such a lofty goal, and they're much less likely to back the project as a result. The lower the funding goal, the more inviting the project is to potential backers.

When I was calculating the funding goal for Viticulture, I asked myself a few key questions:

a. **What is the minimum amount of money I need to raise to make this project a reality?** This involves detailed budgeting based on manufacturer minimums, artists, graphic designers, freight shipping, individual shipping, and processing fees (approximately 8–10 percent of total funding).

b. **What is the amount of money I'm willing to personally invest in the project (or have already invested in it)?** You don't need a fully illustrated board game to launch a crowdfunding project, but you do need at least a few marquee pieces of art that reflect the tone and aesthetic of the game.

c. **How much wiggle room should I leave for when things go wrong?** Inevitably, something unexpected will happen in the design, manufacturing, or fulfillment process. There is also the possibility that the project will be much more successful than I projected, and I need to be ready to scale up.

These questions lead to a basic formula: *funding goal* $= (a - b) + c$

For example, if I need \$40,000 to cover the manufacturing costs of a minimum print run of 1,500 board games, have already invested (or have plans to invest) \$10,000 in art and design, and want to leave a \$5,000 buffer to make up for any unforeseen circumstances, my funding goal would be \$35,000.

If you feel like the result of your calculation is too high, take a close look at your product and try to figure out whether there are any extraneous elements that could be removed, at least temporarily. Offer a core product that you can stand behind, and then create stretch goals that enhance the product if you overfund. That can help you keep the funding goal as low as possible to increase your chances of success.

Stay Focused

Stay focused on what you're raising money for. Stay focused on the audience you're creating it for. Stay focused on what you're trying to deliver to backers.

Why does focus matter? Because every time you lose focus—whether it's in your rewards, on your project page, in your updates, or elsewhere—you dilute your primary objective. If a potential backer looks at your project page for the first time because he wants to buy your game and he has to weed through five pledge levels before he can find the actual game, you may lose that backer. If a potential backer is intrigued by the name of your project, but she can't figure out by looking at your project page what you're raising money for, that's a problem. You're going to lose that backer.

Here's a common example of what I see on those rough draft project pages:

$1	Special thank you on Twitter
$5	Postcard with a photo of us making the game
$15	Art print from the game
$25	T-shirt with our game company logo on it
$49	The game

When I see a reward structure like that, I ask the creator, "What are you trying to sell? Are you in the business of selling art prints? Is your dream to make and ship a handful of T-shirts, or is it your dream to publish a board game?"

If you're trying to raise money to make a board game, the people who come to your project page are there because they want a board game. Stay focused on those potential backers. They're not looking for a postcard, an art print, or a T-shirt, so don't make them weed through all that ancillary junk to get to what they want, and don't spend your precious time creating all that extra stuff when your passion is creating board games. Besides, if a bunch of backers request art prints during your campaign, you can add a pledge level that gets them the game plus the art print. Just don't offer it by itself. Stay focused on your core product.

In terms of dollars and cents, it comes down to this: The success of your $20,000 project to raise money for cat surveillance cameras doesn't hinge on the ten people who choose the $5 postcard level. It hinges on you finding two hundred people to give you $100 each for a cat camera.

Your Target Audience Isn't "Everyone"

When I was preparing to launch Viticulture, I viewed my target audience as evenly split between friends and family, readers of my personal blog, wine lovers, gamers, and people randomly browsing on Kickstarter. I cast a pretty wide net.

I sent out a postproject survey to see whether my prediction was accurate. Figure 8 shows the results.

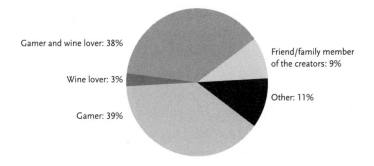

Gamer and wine lover: 38%

Wine lover: 3%

Gamer: 39%

Friend/family member of the creators: 9%

Other: 11%

FIGURE 8. Demographic survey of Viticulture backers.

This is really revealing. Nearly 80 percent of backers were gamers, which in hindsight should have been obvious. Clearly, the people who want to buy board games are gamers. And yes, many of those gamers were also wine lovers, but they were gamers first, then winos. Given the 3 percent of people who were purely wine lovers, I think it's safe to say that the majority of backers in the "gamer and wine lover" category were gamers who happened to love wine.

My point is that it's easy to trick yourself into thinking that *everyone* will want to support your project. And even if they don't, what's the harm in trying to reach everyone? But there are a lot of people in the world, and 99.99 percent of them don't care. If you use your time on that 99.99 percent, you won't have time to reach out to the sliver of a fraction of a percentage who do. You'll also end up alienating or annoying those who do care.

An example of this misconception is a campaign I followed in the summer of 2013. The project was for a very small subset of people: people who like a specific role-playing game (RPG). Granted, some random RPGers who had never heard of the specific RPG may have been interested in the project, but the main target was—or should have been—people who loved that specific platform and universe.

However, the project creator spent a lot of time on the project page explaining some terminology that all RPGers know. His intent was to use inclusive language to make the project accessible to anyone, and that's a good idea—he "made it about them," as I discussed earlier. But "them" in this case was a very specific group of people who already knew the basics of role playing, and they had to plow through those lengthy explanations to get to the information they wanted.

It's our tendency as creators to try to include everyone, and there are certainly ways to do that without alienating your target audience (use the FAQ section, for example). But by trying to include everyone, you lose focus on those who care the most, the people who give you the best chance of succeeding.

This applies not just to the content on the project page but also (and perhaps more importantly) to your marketing efforts and blogger outreach. You might think that a million people want your game, but who are the one thousand most-likely people to actually back it during the campaign? *Figure out who those people are and focus on them.*

Sure, there are tons of blogs out there in every industry that you could reach out to. But your time is limited, and many of those blogs may not be related to or interested in your specific product. Focus on your favorite blogs, whose writers and audiences will get excited to get the inside scoop from you.

I faced this dilemma myself when preparing to launch my campaign for Euphoria, a game about building a dystopia. I had a critical decision to make: do I focus only on gamers, or do I also try to tap into the massive audience of dystopian literature lovers?

I decided to focus solely on gamers. I plugged the dystopian angle among those gamers, but I didn't try to convert any non-gamer dystopian lit readers into gamers. My reason: it isn't the right game. Euphoria isn't a gateway game. If it were a lighter game that might appeal to the average reader of *The Hunger Games*, absolutely, I would have tweeted Suzanne Collins. But rather than spend my time selling a complex game to nongamers, I decided to spend that time connecting with my existing backers.

Make Your Company Sound As Small As You Are

Have you ever heard a sole proprietor or individual entrepreneur refer to themselves as "we"? As in, "We're hoping to launch in about a month." If you ask why the entrepreneur said "we," the answer is almost always that she wants to make her company seem bigger than it actually is to convey *professionalism* and *competence*.

On crowdfunding, smaller is better. Backers connect much more with an individual pursuing his or her passion than with a company asking for preorders. The project page should still be extremely polished—that's where the professionalism and competence comes in—but your individual voice should be heard throughout the text (and even the video). You want to come across as a human, not an industrial machine.

One of the best—and easi- est—ways to convey your size is through the profile photo you use for crowdfunding, Facebook, Twitter, and all other forms of social media. When I was running the Viticulture campaign, I posted from time to time on the Stonemaier Games Facebook page. I read every comment posted there and tried to respond as often as possible.

STONEMAIER
GAMES

FIGURE 9. Stonemaier Games logo.

There is one particular moment I recall from a conversation I was having on the Facebook page with some backers. I think we were talking about what games we were playing that weekend. Every time I posted a comment, the Stonemaier Games logo (fig. 9) appeared next to it.

The more I saw that thumbnail pop up next to comments I was making, the more uncomfortable I became. I felt separated from the comments I was making. Not to mention that the other people involved in the conversation had thumbnails of their faces. It was like I was some faceless corporation, even though I alone run the day-to-day operations at Stonemaier Games. It didn't feel personal at all.

So I changed the thumbnail to what you see in Figure 10. I instantly felt better. The logo is still there, but now it's me, not a corporation, responding to comments on Facebook. I felt like me again.

But really, this isn't about how I feel—it's about how Kickstarter backers feel. How personal should you—the project creator—be with your backers?

The problem with a strictly professional project is that backers can't sense the passion behind the project. They need someone to

FIGURE 10. My Kickstarter and company Facebook page profile photo.

root for—without that shared excitement and passion, they're not likely to share the project with others even if they back it themselves.

Perhaps most importantly, the human element of a project creates *empathy* between the backers and the creator. That's where the photo comes in. Showing your face on your project page in multiple areas will significantly increase the amount of empathy backers feel for you—in fact, I have the data to prove it.

In Daniel Pink's book *To Sell Is Human*, he spends a few pages talking about a very illuminating study involving the power of the human face.[2] Radiologists have the highly impersonal job of looking at anonymous X-rays all day. Usually they're looking for something in particular—a broken bone, for example. But they also save many lives by identifying "incidental findings." For example, while looking at a broken arm, they might notice an odd growth on your rib cage and report it to your doctor.

A few years ago a study was done regarding the effect of including a patient's personal photograph with their X-rays on the rate of incidental findings the radiologists identified. The results were astonishing—when the patient's photograph was included, radiologists discovered 80 percent more incidental findings. 80 percent!

Why the huge jump? The study attributed it to the empathy generated by putting a face to the X-ray: "Our study emphasizes approaching the patient as a human being and not as an anonymous case study," *ScienceDaily* reported.

Sound familiar? As a project creator, let backers see your project *as an extension of you* by showing your face. Let them empathize with you. Let them relate to you and share your passion. Let them see your smiling face in the X-ray that is your project page.

Keep the Campaign Short

Another way that small campaigns win big is in the actual length of the campaign. Kickstarter, for example, permits projects to last between one and sixty days—you choose the duration before you launch. Intuitively you might think that a longer campaign will translate into more backers and more funding. If a thirty-day project raises $30,000, wouldn't a sixty-day project raise $60,000?

The answer: not at all. In fact, a sixty-day project might raise *less* than the thirty-day amount. The key is urgency. A campaign is a launch pad for creation, but the reason crowdfunding works so well is that it gives backers a limited amount of time to make a decision. The longer the time frame, the less urgency your potential backers will feel. Urgency is good—urgency inspires action. This is the same concept used by dating apps like Coffee Meets Bagel and Tinder, which give members a short window of time to make a decision and meet up with their match.

John Coveyou of Genius Games reinforces this idea in a study that uses data from thousands of Kickstarter projects (fig. 11).

The most important piece of data here is the huge drop in the daily pledge average between campaigns that run from twenty-nine to thirty-five days and campaigns between thirty-six and sixty days. Let's do the math: say you're deciding between a thirty-day campaign and a forty-five-day campaign. On average, you will raise a total of $4,451 on the *shorter* campaign compared with only $1,999 on the longer campaign. That's a significant difference.

So what's the right project length for you? If you're a first-time

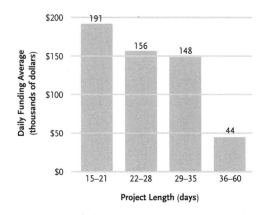

FIGURE 11. A longer project doesn't always result in more funding.

project creator, I recommend that you run a thirty-five-day campaign. That gives more people a chance to discover your project, and more time for you to get it right. You'll need the extra time. If this isn't your first rodeo, run a twenty-five to thirty-day campaign. You've probably honed your skills and are more prepared this time around, so you can shave off a week from your first project. With luck, you'll still capture the majority of people who want to support you, and by saving a week on the project, that's one week you'll save on production.

If you're a serial creator with a large built-in fan base, run an eighteen- to twenty-five-day campaign. That's a pretty broad range, but it depends largely on the type of product and how complete it is. If it's 85 percent complete and you're looking for lots of feedback, run a twenty-five-day campaign. If the product is 100 percent final, aim for eighteen to twenty days. For an established creator, the vast majority of existing fans will know about the campaign on the first day. You want to leave it open for new backers to discover it, but most of the hype surrounding the project will hit in the first few days instead of being spread out over the campaign, as for other projects.

Scarcity Sells

It's basic economics: The lower the supply, the higher the demand. Less is more compelling than, well, *more*. Crowdfunding platforms allow creators to designate each reward either as a limited or unlimited reward.

Author and blogger Seth Godin used this method of scarcity on a 2012 Kickstarter campaign for his book *The Icarus Deception*,[3] which ended up overfunding quite a bit, with $287,342 from 4,242 backers. (Disclaimer: Godin has a massive fan base, so please do not expect to fund your book project at the same level as his project.)

Every one of the project's twelve reward levels was limited, with limits ranging from five backers for a $1,150 reward for which Godin would interview you and write at least one paragraph in the book about "something brave or powerful or remarkable you've done or built," to ten thousand backers for a $4 digital edition of the book. Many sold out within hours of launching.

The day after the project launched, Godin wrote the following on his blog:

> Scarcity cuts both ways. I stated from the beginning that my goal wasn't to maximize the revenue generated from the page, and it was clear within minutes that many readers were excited to be part of something that was limited. Of course, some people got upset by the very same thing—it's hard to balance scarcity (a signed edition, say) with abundance (spreading ideas far and wide).[4]

Here Godin touches upon how the method of scarcity can seem manipulative toward backers, especially if it's *artificial* scarcity. However, if you're looking out for backers' best interests, there is another reason to place limits on certain rewards: The limits give you control over how many units you have to make based on what you can reasonably manufacture and ship. The limits increase your likelihood of fulfilling the promises you made to backers during the project.

Dennis Caco of The Undress project touched on this in the comments section of my crowdfunding blog when I applauded his strategy for offering almost only limited reward levels on his project. The Undress, a dress that allows the wearer to change clothes in public without getting naked, successfully funded in November 2014 with $615,663 from 7,297 backers. Here's what Dennis had to say about the power of scarcity: "We limited our rewards to keep things manageable and keep tabs on all of it—we add quantities as needed as long as we feel confident we can fulfill the orders in a timely manner as promised to our backers."

Dennis is referring to a creator's ability to add new reward levels during the project. I recommend starting with five to seven reward levels and expanding them as needed. Avoid duplicating previously limited reward levels, though, as it devalues the support of those who initially pledged at those levels.

Reasonable Core Reward Anchor Prices and the Premium Option

Similar to how you want to select a reasonable funding goal to make the project inviting to potential backers, it's also important to keep the core reward price as low as possible. Reward-based crowdfunding is not charity. If you overinflate reward prices, it's disrespectful to backers and they won't respond well to your campaign. If people are supporting your dream project, you should offer them a fair value. After all, they're pledging their hard-earned money to something that won't even exist for six to twelve months—the least you can do is offer them a discount on the eventual retail price for the product.

Creating a low core reward price also serves the purpose of framing an "anchor price" to which backers compare all the other special rewards, particularly what I call the "premium option." The premium option is a separate reward that is tantalizingly close to the anchor reward but *so* much better. It offers people a truly compelling reason to spend a little more money to get a significant upgrade. This is good for backers because they get something special and because it gives them an opportunity to pledge a little more money toward the campaign to help it reach some appealing stretch goals.

Michael Coe, president of Gamelyn Games and creator of seven successful crowdfunding projects (nearly $900,000 raised on Kickstarter), has perfectly executed the premium option on several projects. On his Tiny Epic Galaxies tabletop game campaign ($411,693 raised from 12,458 backers in January and February 2015), Michael offered a $16 reward level for a copy of the game—a no-brainer cost to catch peoples' attention—or a $24 reward level for the game plus a limited-edition miniexpansion. The results are telling: 959 backers pledged to receive the core reward, while over ten times that number backed the premium option (10,098 backers).

I've used several different types of premium options on my campaigns. Note that Tuscany has two different premium options because it is an expansion pack to Viticulture, which necessitated reward levels that appealed to people who already owned Viticulture and those who wanted to buy Viticulture and Tuscany for the first time. I've summarized my approach in this table:

Project	Core Reward Price and Backer Count	Premium Option Price and Backer Count	Premium Option Description
Viticulture	$39 61 backers	$49 427 backers	Kickstarter-exclusive expansion
Euphoria	$49 2,314 backers	$59 1,794 backers	Extra set of dice and alternate-art recruit cards
Tuscany	$45 207 backers	$59 596 backers	Seventy-two custom metal lira coins
Tuscany and Viticulture	$79 492 backers	$99 2,833 backers	Seventy-two custom metal lira coins and individually numbered slipcase to contain both games
Treasure Chest	$33 1,792 backers	$39 441 backers	"Early adopter" shipping
Between Two Cities	$29 1,700 backers	$39 3,132 backers	14 city tokens, an individually numbered, gold-foil embossed box, and rules in English, French, and German

If you use the strategy of the premium option, once during the campaign send a message to all backers of the anchor price (Kickstarter allows creators to send mass e-mails to all backers within each reward level) with your best pitch on why they should upgrade to the premium option. Don't be pushy. Just let them know the option is there. Do this exactly once, about three to four days before the end of the campaign, and consider the following:

- **Write the message as though you're writing to one person, not everyone** When a backer gets a message from you, they're much more likely to read it if it is written to an individual, not a group. Don't start with "Hello everyone!" Credit to Michael Domeny on the League of Gamemakers blog for this advice.[5]

- **Be grateful** Thank the backer for making the project a reality.

- **Tell the backer that the project is ending soon**   That's the main point of this message—the backer's ability to order the premium option will expire in a few days.

- **Instruct the backer on how to change his or her pledge**   You do this by clicking the blue Manage Your Pledge button on the project page and manually changing the dollar amount at the top of the page (or the reward level, if applicable). Many backers appreciate the instructions on how to do this, as it's not intuitive for new users.

- **Assure the backer that his or her pledge is great just the way it is**   Because it is. If a backer wants to upgrade, he now has the information he needs to do so, but he appreciates not being pressured to pay more.

Brevity on the Project Page

If you encounter a long paragraph of text online, you are significantly more likely to skim it or even skip it than you are a short paragraph or a graphic. Thus I recommend the following rules for composing your project page:

1. **Keep paragraphs to a maximum of three lines**   I've found that creating a project page months before launch and poking at it a few times a week can eventually turn five- to six-line paragraphs to paragraphs with two or three lines.

2. **Use lists with bolded subject lines**   Lists are much easier to parse than long paragraphs. I typically try to keep each item on the list to two lines or less.

3. **Limit each pledge level to a maximum of eight lines** Reward levels are the most important aspect of your project page. They should be clear, concise, and nonrepetitive.

List the most important or unique aspect at the beginning of each reward level's description. Here's an example from my Treasure Chest campaign of the format I recommend (this is for the $33 reward level):

TREASURE—1 copy of the complete Treasure Chest with all stretch goals. Free shipping & customs for the US, CA, UK, DE, CN, & TW; see shipping chart for other areas. Extra copies are $33. Unavailable via traditional distribution (MSRP would be $60).

4. **Mix text and landscape images**   A great way to break up longer sections of text is to insert one image for every four or six lines of text. I recommend using a program like Adobe InDesign to compile multiple images into one landscape image (like the Tuscany example in figure 12) to reduce the amount of vertical space they occupy on the project page.

FIGURE 12. Landscapified image from the Tuscany project page showing many of the prototype components.

5. **When possible, use infographics**   A well-designed infographic can convey paragraphs of text in one succinct package. These might explain how the product is used. Soberdough has a great example of this on its project page, and so does The Undress project.

All of these techniques combined are sure to make your project page as welcoming as possible to potential backers, which translates into funding for you.

Limiting Project Creep

Projects that start small and focused can spin out of your control if you're not careful about project creep. For example, some projects start out with a lot of add-ons, but perhaps the worst culprits are those that accumulate more and more add-on options during the campaign. This preys on backers' "completionist" tendencies—they want all the things! The solution is to create some new add-ons during the campaign to keep the momentum and excitement, but limit them to one a week at most.

Some projects start off with a few pledge levels, but as the project grows, more and more rewards are added, and the right sidebar becomes bloated with options. Not only is this confusing for people looking for the "complete" game, but if you keep adding more, the backers become jaded about whether the project creator knows what "complete" means. Limit yourself to ten total reward levels for the entire project, so pick and choose new rewards carefully.

Other projects are constantly asking backers for their opinion. Now, I love polls and surveys—they're a great way to engage backers—but everything can't be up for discussion, and after a certain point backers get tired of polls and just want you to make up your mind already! Limit yourself to one poll a week, and be clear about when the poll will close. Remember to share the results.

Excessive calls to action are probably the most common example of project creep. Some projects constantly ask backers to share, Like, tweet, thumb, and the like. Backers start to wonder, "Is it ever enough?" It's important to empower backers with specific, creative ways to share the project, but limit these requests to no more than one update a week. And definitely don't do this or encourage it in the comments section. You can kill a vibrant backer discussion really fast if someone—the creator or a backer—is constantly telling backers to go share the project.

And no matter how excited you are that your project is actually happening, don't drown backers in updates! Save up until you have something really important to say, then say it in one update, putting any ancillary information at the bottom of the post. Don't write an update on consecutive days unless it's absolutely imperative that backers read it right away. The best way to learn about the pitfalls of project updates is to subscribe to a project yourself and follow the updates until you get so annoyed with them that you unsubscribe. Jot down why you unsubscribed, and then make sure you don't do the same thing when you run your project.

Your backers have already done *so* much for you by becoming backers in the first place. Respect and retain them by limiting project creep.

There are a myriad of ways that going small and focusing on backers helps creators win big. From reasonable funding goals to discounted reward pricing to the structure of the project page itself, creators can significantly improve their chances of success by prioritizing the little things.

CHAPTER 9

Build a Better Community

Viticulture raised $65,980 on Kickstarter from 942 backers in October 2012. Seven months later, Euphoria raised $309,495 from 4,765 backers. That's a 500 percent increase. How does that happen?

The answer, I believe, is something I've identified in almost every project that wildly overfunds. It's all about *building community*. The community you build before the project will often support you financially or on social media. The community you build during the project will invite others to join them and will elevate the quality of the product. And the community you build after the project will be your product's biggest fans and advocates.

Every chapter in this book talks about ways to build community, from the steps you take to connect with people who share your passion months before your project launches, to the backer-centric focus during the project, to postproject communication and updates.

A great example of a creator who builds community is Brad Martin of Webster City, Iowa. Brad runs a company called Tactical Keychains, which specializes in custom-crafted metal accessories like the titular keychains, bottle openers, and pens. I had never heard of Brad until I asked my backers to tell me about their favorite project creators. Despite the vast sea of crowdfunding projects out there, Brad's name came up multiple times.

Brad's crowdfunding campaigns have a distinct look and feel to them that I wouldn't necessarily recommend to other creators, but they fit Brad's ebullient personality. They're full of exclamation marks, positive remarks from blogs and magazines, and smiley faces. Brad keeps his funding goals small (usually $999) because the way he manufacturers his products doesn't require a high minimum threshold, and as a result, the *lowest* any of his campaigns have overfunded is 1,702 percent above the goal.

It's tough to represent Brad's distinctive voice by writing about it, so I'll let him describe his approach to building community. It's less a strategy and more a default mode for Brad:

> I just treat everyone like family, they are supporting me so I support them when I can. I have the best backers on Kickstarter, some of them have even flown to other backers locations and hung out with them! I've connected many people from all over the world, traded e-mail addresses and even started our own forum to just chat. I've gotten PayPal from people for my birthday, or gift cards to go out and eat with my wife, books, and many other things delivered, the list goes on. It's almost like a dream.
>
> I let the backers have a say in what we do, and then throw them up as stretch goals. It's hard on some projects, but I try. Look at my TiPeN project, over 16,000 comments—that was a blast! There is always over 1,000 comments on my projects :)

To Brad, backers aren't customers. They're family. They feel a strong connection to Brad, so they return to his projects time after time.

Addressing the Mid-campaign Slump with Inward-Facing Community Building

It's fairly common for crowdfunding projects to hit a mid-campaign slump. There's a lot of enthusiasm and excitement for the first week, and then it dies down and pledges start to trickle in. That's okay—your project isn't dead.

Your instinct might be to try to find quick fixes for the lull. You start spamming Facebook with pleas for support. You consider disingenuous cross-promotion offers from other projects. You're tempted by campaign-boosting services.

The problem with those methods of reinvigorating your campaign is that they're *outward-facing*. That is, you're overlooking your most powerful asset: your current backers. Out of seven billion people in the world, a few hundred of them have decided to pledge to your project. That's a big deal! They are your most powerful advocates and supporters. If you nurture your relationship with backers, their influence will spread beyond the campaign itself. If you neglect them, even they will leave you behind.

End Every Project Update with a Question

This is one of the easiest ways to start the conversations that build community. Simply by ending a project update with a specific question for backers (not a yes-or-no question), you will convert the update from a *diatribe* into a *dialogue*.

Listen and Act on Backer Comments

Your fantastic backers will share their thoughts about the project with you whether or not you ask for their input. One percent of the things they tell you are silly and will bankrupt you. The other 99 percent is really good advice, even if it's advice you're not ready to hear.

Are backers complaining about shipping prices? Find a better fulfillment solution. Are they complaining about the illustrations? Find a better artist. Sometimes these fixes require rebooting the project. But some of them can be done on the fly. Not only will current backers feel valued that you listened and implemented their advice, but your project will be more attractive to potential backers as well.

Engage Backers through Polls That Shape the Product

Backers feel valued when they're a part of the decision-making process. Some backers are very vocal about their opinions, but those voices can distort the true feeling of the majority. Polls are a great way to mitigate the vocal minority.

On his board game project Burning Suns ($142,985 raised from 1,313 backers),[1] Emil Larsen used polls to let backers select their favorite spaceship design for each of the alien races in the game. Not only do backers feel more invested in the project after participating in a poll like this, but—if democracy serves you well—you will end up with the most appealing version of the product.

Streamline and Add Reward Levels

It might be time to do some spring cleaning on your reward levels. The first thing to do is look for rewards that no one has backed. Remove those levels—there's a reason no one has backed them, and they're diluting the rest of your rewards. You can also add reward levels, especially if backers frequently ask for them.

On both my Euphoria and Treasure Chest campaigns, backers kept requesting that I add a special $59 reward level (extra dice and alternate-art cards for Euphoria; a combo pack of treasure, stars, and coins on the Treasure Chest). It took me a week or so both times to be convinced that it was the right move, but in the end, the backers were right. The new level on Euphoria attracted 1,794 backers, and the new Treasure Chest reward drew 798 backers.

Whenever you make a change like this based on backer input,

it injects tangible enthusiasm into the project—comment participation will increase, and many backers will upgrade their pledge, giving the project a much-needed financial bump.

Secret Philanthropists

Many creators don't have the luxury of having friends with deep pockets, but if you do, there's a way those donors can inject much more than just funds into your campaign.

In 2012, a video game project called Tex Murphy—Project Fedora ($598,104 raised from 6,963 backers) inspired backers to continually check in on the funding goal by teasing them with the idea that seven secret philanthropists were poised to pledge $5,000 to the project whenever funding hit certain unrevealed levels. Backers wanted to be there every time the funding jumped by $5K. In the meantime, they hung out in the comments section, talking with one another about the project. By the end of the campaign, there were over 24,000 comments on the main page.

Give Backers a Visual Challenge

Midway through the crowdfunding campaign for the board game Lift Off! ($50,462 raised from 1,014 backers), Eduardo Baraf attended the big gaming convention in Indianapolis called Gen Con. Convention presence during a campaign can sometimes decrease backer engagement, as you're not as available to moderate and participate in the comments section.

However, Eduardo used this time to his advantage by giving away his distinct alien tokens to anyone who wanted to take a photo of them doing something mischievous at the convention. The result was a delightful mashup of the little aliens invading events, locations, and other games—backers had a lot of fun with it (fig. 13).

FIGURE 13. Photos of alien meeples from the Lift Off! game. Reproduced courtesy of Eduardo Baraf.

Give Backers a Mystery to Solve

People love a good mystery, especially if it makes them feel clever. There are a few ways this method can be used to build community among backers. The first is to offer thematic riddles in project updates as Aerjen Tamminga did in his project Pleasant Dreams: A Card Game of Nightmares ($11,327 raised from 604 backers).[2] By ending project updates with riddles, Aerjen created an opportunity for backers to engage in the project and with one another (fig. 14).

The other way is to have a mystery that runs throughout the entire project. This is a common literary device often used on scripted television: each episode is self-contained, but viewers return from week to week to learn more about the season-long, overarching mystery. It works with crowdfunding too.

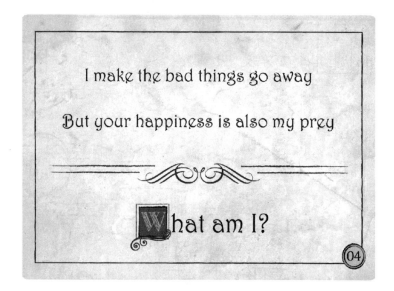

I make the bad things go away

But your happiness is also my prey

What am I?

04

FIGURE 14. One of the clues from the puzzle on the Pleasant Dreams campaign. Reproduced courtesy of Aerjen Tamminga.

Addressing the Mid-campaign Slump with Outward-Facing Community Building

What do you do if you're midway through a project and you realize that your existing audience isn't enough? Even if you're doing a great job at engaging backers and building community on the crowdfunding platform, you might need to extend your reach beyond that to attract new backers.

Change Your Approach to Reaching Out to Blogs and Podcasts

Bloggers and podcasters need content, and they're always looking to expand their audience. If they're not replying to your requests, it's probably because you're doing it wrong. Reaching out to bloggers and saying, "Hey, talk about my project!" isn't going to get you anywhere. Instead, show each blogger and podcaster you target that you know their audience and can provide interesting, relevant content to that audience. The hidden lesson is that this isn't about promoting your project—it's about adding value to bloggers and podcasters and then promoting *their* content.

Hang Out, but Don't Promote

If you spend your time on Facebook, Twitter, or any form of media, just hang out. Relax. Chat. Discuss. Debate. *Don't promote*. Promotion is about pushing your agenda onto other people whether they want to hear it or not. It's unattractive and off-putting, and it will drive people away. Conversely, hanging out is all about making friends. It's a lot more fun than promoting, and the people who share your passion will gravitate toward you. How will they know you have an active crowdfunding campaign? If you've done your job getting the word out to bloggers, they'll know.

Paid Advertising

It might seem odd to pay for advertising for something that doesn't exist yet, but sometimes it can make a huge difference in a project's chance of success. Target a few websites with audiences that are likely to be interested in your product. Make sure to include some sense of urgency in the banner ad so that potential backers know they have a limited time to make a pledge.

Make One to Two Calls to Action

Once or twice during your project, post a project update in which you ask backers to recommend the project to one friend. Not all of their friends; *one* friend. Make it easy for them to select that friend. For example, for the Blank Slate Press campaign, I might have said,

"Please share this project with the friend of yours who gives the best book recommendations." Making a specific request like that will help the backer target one person who might actually be interested in the project instead of spamming all of their Facebook friends.

Send Personal Appeals Asking Friends and Family

The key word here is *personal*. Do not send a mass e-mail to everyone in your address book. It's simply not effective—it's spam, and people ignore spam. People are significantly more willing to act if it's clear that you personally appealed to them instead of lumping them into the ubiquitous sludge of a mass e-mail. Instead, send individual messages to people containing the following:

- Tell the person why you thought to contact them specifically, connecting that reason to your project.

- Ask them a genuine, specific question to show them that this isn't all about you.

- Request that they check out the project by clicking the link you included. Don't ask for money.

- If you think they don't know what crowdfunding is, explain it to them. This is an opportunity to teach.

Create and Share News of Microgoals

People like to see and reach milestones, no matter how much they actually matter. For example, would you be happier if you were the backer that got a project to reach $9,957 or the one to get it to reach $10,000 (out of a $20,000 funding goal)? $10,000, right? Give people a reason to make an immediate difference on your project, even if that difference is an irrelevant number (dollars or number of backers).

This method turned around the Torn Armor miniatures game project,[3] which was trending toward unsuccessful funding until the creator, Natalya Alyssa Faden, started implementing a system of microgoals.[4] Torn Armor eventually reached and exceeded its funding goal of $50,000, raising $67,742 from 561 backers.

The Matching Pledge

As any development director for a nonprofit will tell you, a matching gift is one of the most powerful tools for getting people to give and engage. I'm much more likely to donate if my gift of $50 will turn into $100 thanks to a generous donor. It's just as powerful on crowdfunding, where sometimes you need a better reason than stretch goal enhancements to encourage backers to share the project with their friends.

That's the approach that David Montgomery and Marcelo Vital took with their graphic novel project, *The Secret Around-the-World Adventures of Owney the Postal Dog* ($10,340 raised from 142 backers).[5] When the project had just over $4,000 in funding, David and Marcelo announced that a generous backer was going to match all pledges received ($1,200 maximum) over a two-day period. It inspired current backers to upgrade their pledges and share the project with their friends, and it gave any friends and family members who were on the fence a reason to back now instead of later. An even more prominent example of this was Seth MacFarlane's commitment to match every pledge dollar to dollar between the $4 million and $5 million funding marks on the Reading Rainbow project ($5,408,916 raised from 105,857 backers).

These aren't the only methods for generating buzz during a campaign, but they're a good start. Your success will depend on a combination of the methods I've described and what's best for your particular project.

Getting Back to the Roots

Two creators who personify the concept of building community through Kickstarter are Nikhil Arora and Alejandro Velez of Back to the Roots in Oakland, California. When they were wrapping up their college experience at UC Berkeley, they learned about a method of growing gourmet mushrooms from recycled coffee grounds. Inspired by the prospect of turning waste into a food source, they developed their first product, the Mushroom Kit.

I stumbled upon Back to the Roots while watching a TEDx Talk by Nikhil and Alex.[6] One particular line captured my attention and summed up their core business model. Nikhil said, "There is so much more value and interchange that can be added to that traditional linear business model that just starts with the supplier and then just ends with the customer." It's the same ideology that first excited me about crowdfunding: the platform creates an opportunity for creators to *collaborate with* customers, not just *sell to* them.

As Back to the Roots grew, Nikhil and Alex started to explore other ideas for sustainable products that allowed people to grow their own food. It was with that goal in mind that they invented the Aquafarm, an aquarium with a garden built into the lid. It's a self-contained ecosystem in which the plants on top of the aquarium clean the water, the water provides nutrients for the plants, and the fish feed off the plants.

Despite the relationships they had built through the Mushroom Kit, they found that retailers were hesitant to commit to orders for an unproven product. So, despite some concerns about how customers would perceive an established business like Back to the Roots seeking crowdfunding, they turned to Kickstarter in November 2012.

While creating and running their Kickstarter campaign for the Home Aquaponics Kit,[7] Nikhil and Alex focused on the core philosophy that had made their business successful: they viewed backers as partners. They acted on this by bouncing ideas off their backers throughout the campaign, actively seeking feedback about how people would use the Aquafarm and tweaking the design accordingly.

When I spoke to Nikhil a year and a half after the campaign ended, he elaborated on how they viewed backers. "What we owe to backers is more than early access and discounts," he said." "They were fully invested in the journey of the Aquafarm and the Back to the Roots mission, so we saw our role as satisfying their emotional needs." He went on to cite Maslow's hierarchy of needs (physiological, safety, social, esteem, and self-actualization). I like to hear a crowdfunder talk about their backers in such a nurturing, loving way.

Did their method of building community work? Of course it did—that's why I'm writing about it! The Home Aquaponics Kit raised $248,873 from 4,097 backers. That's a staggering amount for any project, and back in 2012, they were among a rare crop of projects to exceed the $200,000 mark.

"Community" isn't a static concept. It starts before a project, grows during the campaign, and blossoms—or withers—afterward. Nikhil and Alex had to stay on top of their game after the campaign because the feedback they incorporated into the Aquafarm added three months to the production schedule. They kept backers informed and engaged throughout the process. When the product shipped, many backers received a faulty pump. Maintaining their view that backers are partners and not one-time, disposable wallets, Nikhil and Alex shipped thousands of new pumps to backers. This hurt profitability in the short-term, but catching the mistake before a broader retail production run prevented a much bigger problem from happening later. In fact, when they released a second version of the Aquafarm in 2014, they reached out to backers and offered them a special upgrade kit at cost (plus shipping)—their sense of gratitude extended well beyond the original campaign.

As a business that started with two college graduates and has grown to a company with fifteen employees, Back to the Roots has proved that a community-centric approach can lead to a huge amount of success for Kickstarter and beyond.

ABS: Always Be Subscribing

You can't build a community—particularly an online community—if you don't have a platform for doing so. The crowdfunding website *is* that platform during the campaign, but what about before and after the project?

By far the most important platform is your e-newsletter. There is no better way to directly connect with every person who cares about your company. Facebook posts are seen by only a small percentage of fans, and tweets are fleeting. But when you send out an e-newsletter, all subscribers see it.

The power of the e-newsletter comes with great responsibility. Send the e-newsletter once a month, with the only exception being when you have something important and time-sensitive to announce. Also be sure that the subject line and the first paragraph of the e-newsletter contain the most important content you want people to read. Do not automatically subscribe all backers to your e-newsletter—that's illegal. Offer backers the option to opt in. And make sure that all subscribers (especially backers) save the e-mail address you use to send your e-newsletter in their contacts list so that it doesn't go to spam. You want to minimize the number of subscribers who miss out on important notifications.

An e-newsletter is the best way to build a community online, but it's not the only way. Here are the primary purposes of the most important platforms:

- **E-newsletter**   The best way to reach all of the people who are interested in what you and your company are doing (I use MailChimp).

- **Blog/podcast**   Sharing your personality and creating conversations

- **Facebook page**   Sharing photos and miniupdates; engaging people through casual conversation

- **YouTube**   Visual content and sharing your personality (Instagram and Pinterest are also driven by visuals, albeit static ones, not video)

- **Twitter**   Fleeting topics that only a few will see; engaging people in a very casual way, often about their topics of choice

Use a balanced strategy when building community on these platforms. That is, don't post the same thing at the same time on every form of social media. Stagger different types of posts across all platforms, and where applicable, be an active participant in the comments section.

Building a Better Dystopian Community

Back to the original question: How did I grow my community (and project funding) by 500 percent from Viticulture to Euphoria?

In addition to designing Euphoria, I spent seven months building two communities: the Viticulture backer community and the community of crowdfunding creators. Viticulture backers were my top priority. This was my first board-game campaign, and I wanted to get it right by firmly establishing a foundation of trust with those backers. I kept backers in the loop through project updates, and I continued to make little tweaks throughout the process with backers' best interests at heart (like changing one of the player colors in the game to make it more friendly for color-blind users).

I delivered Viticulture early to many backers in Asia and Australia, then I shipped most of the remaining games just before I launched the Euphoria campaign. The idea that we could deliver as promised (and create a beautiful product) was fresh on backers' minds.

If I had done nothing more than focus on Viticulture backers, the Euphoria campaign would have still been successful. But I believe that it was my focus on adding value to other creators through my Kickstarter Lessons blog (and thus making crowdfunding better for backers, too) that created an overall sense in the gaming industry that I was there to give, not take.

Of course, that's a subjective statement that's tough to quantify. The numbers from Euphoria's first forty-eight hours are telling, though, as they reflect the large number of people who were poised and ready to back the project right away despite not knowing much about the game before that day. It also helped that our e-newsletter list had swelled to over 1,500 people at that point. In the first forty-eight hours, Euphoria raised $47,930 (compared with a $15,000 goal) from 771 backers—it was already encroaching on Viticulture's funding total (for a forty-two-day campaign).

Granted, it isn't unusual for a creator to return to crowdfunding and experience a strong first few days. A lot went into making the project appealing to backers: bright, attractive, distinctive art from Jacqui Davis; custom dice; a long list of stretch goals; our money-back guarantee; and free shipping to the United States, Canada, and the EU. But without a strong community of people who are ready and eager to back your project from day 1, projects that have been more inviting and better looking than Euphoria have fallen flat.

CHAPTER 10

Don't Quit Your Day Job ...
Until You Quit Your Day Job

It's tempting to quit your day job after a successful crowdfunding project—I've been there. After Euphoria raised more than $300,000 in June 2013, I seriously considered making it my full-time focus right away. At the time, I was working ninety plus hours a week: forty at my day job, and fifty plus on Stonemaier.

But, that's the dream, right? Doing something you love, being creative, interacting with people who share your passions. Who wouldn't want to do that full-time every day, especially with $300K in the bank?

The truth is, you're probably going to need every penny of those Kickstarter funds to manufacture and ship your product. The choice is yours: do you put your backers first and use those funds to deliver on your promises, or do you use those funds for everyday living expenses?

How to Doom Your Project in One Easy Step

There is an infamous crowdfunding project called The Doom That Came to Atlantic City that successfully funded on June 6, 2012, for a total of $122,874. The vast majority of the 1,246 backers pledged $75 or more to receive the game, which had an estimated delivery date of November 2012.

Six months after that, the project had not yet been delivered. On July 23, 2013, backers received the following update from Erik

Chevalier, who had run the Kickstarter campaign. I've removed a few of the paragraphs to condense the lengthy update:[1]

> This is not an easy update to write.
>
> The short version: The project is over, the game is canceled.
>
> After paying to form the company, for the miniature statues, moving back to Portland, getting software licenses and hiring artists to do things like rule book design and art conforming the money was approaching a point of no return. We had to print at that point or never. Unfortunately that wasn't in the cards for a variety of reasons.
>
> My hope now is to eventually refund everyone fully. This puts all of the financial burden directly on my shoulders. Starting with those who've pre-ordered after the Kickstarter campaign through our webstore, then I'll begin working my way through the backer list, starting with those who funded at the highest levels. Unfortunately I can't give any type of schedule for the repayment as I left my job to do this project and must find work again. I'll create a separate bank account to place anything beyond my basic costs of living. Every time that account has a decent amount saved into it I'll issue a payout to a portion of the backer list. I'll post updates with each payout to keep you all informed on the progress.
>
> Sincerest apologies,
> Erik Chevalier

Compounding the fact that Erik incurred the expenses of moving to Portland was his statement about quitting his day job to finish the crowdfunded product. Thousands of board-game projects have been successfully delivered without their creators leaving their day jobs. As a result, in June 2015 the Federal Trade Commission issued a complaint against Chevalier, alleging that he never paid artists and instead spent backer funds purely on personal expenses and licenses for a different project. This sets a precedent that the FTC—not just backers—will hold a creator accountable for misuse of funds.

Creators who eat first finish last.

Time Is Money

The trouble that many creators encounter is that it takes a lot of time to run a business, even if that business has exactly one product. So how do you fulfill the promises to the backers of your successfully funded project and still make money to pay the bills?

- **Don't change anything for as long as possible**   It's that simple. Do both your day job and your crowdfunding job as long as you possibly can. You'll know when you can't do it any longer when your crowdfunding responsibilities encroach so much into your day job that you're no longer giving either the attention they deserve. I did this for about two months after the Euphoria campaign ended.

- **Don't pay yourself**   The money you raised on Kickstarter isn't for your personal enjoyment. However, the nice twist is that if you earmarked $5,000 of your personal savings for the crowdfunding project in case you didn't raise as much as you really needed, and instead you overfunded, treat yourself to something nice with a little bit of those funds. For example, I bought a pair of jeans.

- **Try to reduce your day job hours**   Take a very close look at your personal budget. Look at how much you earn each month and how much you spend each month, and use the difference to calculate your proposed reduction in hours.

So, say you make $4,000 a month, and you spend $3,000 a month. As long as you have some money in savings for unexpected life events, those numbers would indicate that you could reduce your day job hours and salary by 25 percent. Propose the idea to your boss and see what she says. Many bosses are happy to save money. My boss loved the idea, so I stopped working on Wednesdays. Having that one day completely devoted to Stonemaier made a huge difference at a pivotal time.

- **Before doing anything else, produce and deliver the product to backers** This is huge. I don't care how much money you raise—if you haven't delivered the product to your backers, that money means nothing. What if you budgeted $30,000 for shipping and it costs you $50,000? What if the price of cardboard skyrockets and the game costs twice as much to make? What if you get sued? So many things can go wrong during production and shipping. Deliver the product before making any life-changing decisions. I had already delivered most copies of Euphoria before my last day at my full-time job.

- **Create alternative revenue streams and budget for the future** When you really start to think you want to run your business full-time, look toward the future. The revenue from your crowdfunding project was a one-time deal. Sure, you raised $200,000, but you're going to spend the majority of that money on making and delivering the product. How will you earn steady income month to month for the next year or so—not just enough to cover your living expenses, but also to keep enough cash flow to make more copies of your product?

At this point, you might be just fine—you might have found a great balance between your day job and your new business. If so, stick with it. If not, consult with friends, family, and your business partner(s) before taking the next step.

Thank You for Popping

One of my favorite companies created through crowdfunding is Quinn Popcorn. Kristy and Coulter Lewis love microwave popcorn. When they had their first son, Quinn, they started looking closely at the ingredients on the food they bought, including their favorite snack. When they realized the amount of preservatives, chemical coatings, and artificial ingredients in a typical bag of popcorn, they were shocked. They wanted something better for their son and for each other.

So they reinvented the entire concept of microwave popcorn, starting with the bag and ending with the ingredients. They even created flavors not usually found in the grocery store, like parmesan and rosemary, Vermont maple syrup and sea salt, and lemon and sea salt. The result—as I can attest to firsthand—is a truly unique, delicious bag of popcorn.

To make Quinn Popcorn a reality, Coulter and Kristy turned to Kickstarter. It was July 2011, when crowdfunding was in its infancy, but they saw the potential of the platform and wanted to use it to launch their company. Thus, they built plenty of buffer room into their reward pricing to allow for excess funds to go toward scaling up after the campaign. One box of popcorn was $15, or backers could get three boxes for $35.

After thirty days, the campaign successfully overfunded at $27,880 (well above their $10,000 goal) from 755 backers. That may seem like a modest project by today's standards, but back then it was in the upper echelon of projects (particularly food-related projects).

In May 2014 I spoke with Coulter about the experience. On the phone he sounded very busy and out of breath—as he told me, he and his team "bust their asses" every day to make a great product.

During the crowdfunding campaign, the Quinn Popcorn team relied heavily on friends, family, and Kickstarter itself to promote and fund the project. When Coulter and Kristy were packing up the first batch for backer fulfillment, they wanted to write "thank you" on each box of popcorn going to people they knew. However, their popcorn-packing process was separate from their shipping process, so they didn't know to which backer each box of popcorn was going during the first stage. They decided instead to write "thank you" on *every* box they shipped by hand, a tradition they continue to this day for orders made through their website.

Coulter told me that they learned to tell the story of Quinn Popcorn through the project-creation process. You really have to hone your pitch and develop your branding to get attention on Kickstarter, which Coulter and Kristy did by finding ways to create something that people will talk about and share. They studied other projects to see what excited people and what fell flat, and they incorporated those lessons into their project.

As with the original Home Aquaponics Kit, the first batch of Quinn Popcorn wasn't perfect, but backers were already invested in Coulter, Kristy, and the whole idea of pure microwave popcorn. To leverage the insight of the crowd to improve the product in the long run, they created a page on their website specifically for backer feedback. It reads:

> Our first batch is just getting out there. We KNOW there are ways we can make it better next time; we know it's not perfect!
>
> This is where you come in.
>
> We would love to know your thoughts before we produce round two!

Feel free to critique the crap out of it. The good, the bad, EVERYTHING! We can handle it ... I think. 😃

So feel free to post your comments here. Thanks for being awesome!

As Coulter says, "You can't buy honest feedback." But when people have already paid you, the door is open for some great input. Quinn Popcorn used that input to improve the second batch, propelling the company toward the level of success it has achieved today. Despite its humble origins, the company now offers their popcorn in thousands of stores across the United States, including Wegmans, Whole Foods, and Target.

How to Quit Your Day Job in Four Easy Steps

I've now been running Stonemaier Games full-time since December 2013. Time will tell if this is something I can continue to do for years and years, but I've taken intentional steps toward doing this full-time and keeping my backers' best interests at heart.

- **Talk to your family** I'm fortunate to have wonderful parents who have supported me throughout my life. I'll never forget the phone call when I told them I was thinking about leaving my day job to focus full-time on Stonemaier Games. They told me something that made me know I was making the right decision. They said, "Jamey, we love and support you. But we want you to know that we're not going to bail you out financially if this doesn't work out." That was exactly what I needed to hear. I needed to know that I was on my own for this harebrained endeavor. I felt confident in my ability to make ends meet without my parents as a fallback plan, so I knew I was making the right choice.

- **Tell your boss one-on-one before you tell any other coworker**
  Your boss should be the first person at your organization to
  know your decision—you don't want him finding out from
  another employee. Just like a breakup, don't make it about
  your boss or your job—explain that the decision is rooted
  in your passion for your growing company. I debated the
  best way to do this because I was worried about my boss's
  response. After chatting with several friends and family
  members, I decided to tell my boss first—privately—and it
  was absolutely the right decision.

- **Don't burn bridges**   Some people out there truly despise
  their jobs, and it can be really tempting to go out in flames.
  Resist those temptations. People are going to remember you
  by your exit, so exit gracefully and respectfully. I did everything I could to help with the transition—in fact, I still drop
  by my old job when needed to help train people.

- **Coordinate the logistics of your future employment in advance**
  Remember when you started your day job and filled out
  a few forms for human resources to take out your health
  insurance, salary, 401k, life insurance, and the like? Well,
  now *you* are human resources, so you have to do all that
  stuff. Contact your insurance agent for health care, life insurance, and disability insurance. Transfer your 401k to an IRA.
  Figure out a regular schedule to pay yourself from company
  funds. If it's just you, payroll is actually quite easy—you
  don't have to worry about taxes until next year (your salary
  counts as expenses against your company revenue, and your
  accountant will take care of it). Also, if you get a lot of company mail, sign up for a forwarded post office box.

Finally, the day comes when you're working for yourself full-time. This will vary depending on your situation, but many crowd-funders who go full-time will work from home. I've learned a few things about working from the confines of my condo, beyond the obvious bonus of a pants-optional environment.

First, get out of the house once a day. This was my biggest concern when I started working full-time. I'm an introvert, so I'm perfectly happy seeing people only a few times a week. The problem is, I would rapidly become a hermit if I lived that way. Even as an introvert, I need to interact with people (not just my cats) on a regular basis. Plus, I need to do things like wear clothes and shower—I'm more focused on work when I feel like I'm at work, and it's hard to feel that way when I smell like bed. So I've tried to get into the habit of leaving home at least once a day or inviting people over once a day. Sometimes that means not taking care of all my errands on a single run, but for the most part it's meant that I get to play a lot of games with people multiple times a week.

Also, separate work and personal space. I'm single, and I own a two-bedroom condo. For the last year, my second bedroom has been the place where I keep game supplies, and my bedroom has my computer, bed, clothes, and other personal effects. When I started working full-time, I spoke with a professional organizer, who recommended that I completely separate my work and personal spaces. It's important to create a mental and physical divide between the two. So now my bed, clothes, and books are in the small bedroom, and all Stonemaier stuff, my desk, my computer, and my playtest/prototype supplies are in my "office." Someday I might expand into a separate office space, but for now this is all I need.

It's also important to be intentional about work and play. When people learn that I work for myself at home now, the most commonly asked question is, "Is it hard to get work done?" My answer: "It's hard to not do work!" Within minutes of waking up, I'm replying to e-mails, blog comments, social media posts, and so on. Then I'm designing and developing games, coordinating logistics, and planning for our next crowdfunding project. I stop working around midnight. That's sixteen hours of work a day and eight hours of sleep. Rinse, repeat, no weekends. So other than getting out of the office or inviting people over, I try to be really intentional about not constantly working. Sometimes that's a twenty-minute break to play an iPad game, or I watch an extra TV show after eating dinner. And before I go to bed, I make sure to read fiction for at least twenty to thirty minutes because it completely gets my mind off work so that I can sleep well before starting the cycle all over. Everyone has different needs in this area, so figure out what's right for you.

Don't quit your day job. But if you realize that you can afford to live your life and at least test the waters of a career in whatever your crowdfunded company is, I hope this template gives you a starting point.

CHAPTER 11

You Are Your Own Gatekeeper

In Chapter 2, I talked about how the crowd is the new gatekeeper. Now that you've read the book, here's my M. Night Shyamalan twist for you: *you are your own gatekeeper.*

That chapter began with the story of how the Kickstarter campaign for Tuscany: Expand the World of Viticulture—my first project after quitting my day job—raised over $158,000 in the first twenty-four hours (the original funding goal was $20,000). Because of the excess of beautiful components in the game through stretch goals, positive word of mouth, and the reputation we built for excellent customer service, the campaign maintained momentum throughout the twenty-nine days—even on the slowest day of funding we raised $3,753. It helped that the most attractive reward, a Collector's Edition containing Viticulture, Tuscany, and premium metal coins, was $99. As a result, even just a few backers could cause the overall funding to jump in large increments.

At the end of the project in April 2014, Tuscany had raised $450,333 from 4,333 backers. It was then that I truly felt like my own gatekeeper, and I had opened up the gate to the possibility of a career with Stonemaier Games.

Diversification

I wanted to make sure the company was secure enough to sustain me as a full-time employee. At the time, we had two products in distribution—Viticulture (which was between printings) and Euphoria—but we didn't have consistent cash flow to keep the company afloat for the long term. So I brokered a European production partnership for Euphoria with Morning Players in France (and later our other games) and a Chinese production partnership with One Moment Games (fig. 15).

I also tried to diversify our product line with a game accessory called the Treasure Chest. This was an idea inspired by the discussion about the exclusive content in Euphoria (see Chapter 7). I was spoiled by the realistic resource tokens in that game and thought there might be demand for them, so I designed an original set of the tokens (gold, stone, brick, wood, ore, and gems—commonly used resources in a variety of board games) and launched a Kickstarter project in June 2014 (fig. 16).

This was probably the riskiest project I had launched to date because I really didn't know how much demand there was for the

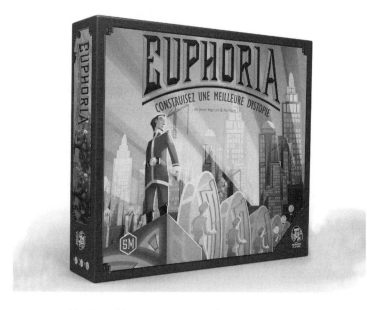

FIGURE 15. The French-language version of Euphoria, produced in coordination with Morning Players.

FIGURE 16. Stonemaier Games Treasure Chest of six different premium tokens to replace generic cubes in many board games.

special tokens. They were expensive to make; in fact, they were so expensive that they would have justified a $55–60 MSRP. That didn't seem like an attractive price point, so we decided to charge $33 on Kickstarter ($39–45 postcampaign) and make the tokens available only directly from Stonemaier Games. We wouldn't enter the product into distribution.

The Treasure Chest crowdfunding campaign was a streamlined, no-frills project. It featured a $25,000 funding goal, simple stretch goals (a new token would be added to every box for every 100 backers), and a short time frame (seventeen days). The core rewards were simple: $33 for one copy of the Treasure Chest delivered in January 2015 or $39 for an air-freighted Treasure Chest to arrive in December for those who wanted it in time for the holidays.

Our gamble paid off with 3,221 happy backers (well, 3,220 happy backers; one backer used the money-back guarantee to return his Treasure Chest for a refund because he thought the red brick tokens were purple) and a total funding of $181,157. That's markedly less than Tuscany, but I think that's okay on crowdfunding. Different products are going to appeal to different people. It's flattering for me to hear backers say, "I'll support anything you create," but I want them to keep me on my toes and selectively pledge to projects that appeal to them.

In addition to the international partnerships and Treasure Chest product, we printed more copies of Euphoria and Viticulture for distribution. We also recognized that the company wouldn't sustain itself with me as the lead designer on all games—running the day-to-day operations takes an increasing amount of time with each SKU we add, so my design time is limited. To address this, we acquired the rights to a game called Between Two Cities from designers Ben Rosset and Matthew O'Malley. It's more of a "gateway game" (an easy-to-learn game that's appealing to people who are new to the hobby) than our other games, which is one of the ways we're trying to diversify our product line.

It's important that I don't lose sight of what originally drew me to this career—my passion for designing games. My current focus is on a game called Scythe, which I'm working on with Polish artist Jakub Rozalski. I was drawn to the alternate-history 1920s Eastern European world Jakub has been building and wanted to design a game in that world. Jakub and I struck up a partnership, and the project is in development as of February 2015 (fig. 17).

I'm working on several more treasure chests while pursuing several games from other designers, as well as creating a Euphoria expansion with designer Morten Monrad Pedersen. I've also solidified the company's legal standing by working with lawyers on contracts and trademarks.

FIGURE 17. Scythe box art by Jakub Rozalski.

The point of all this is that it's important to diversify if you want to turn a successful crowdfunding campaign into an ongoing career.

It's Time to Create

Publishers, newspapers, software firms, producers, game companies—these are just a few examples of the gatekeepers that had the power to decide whether your dream project was worth making.

I have nothing against those companies. Stonemaier Games is becoming one of those companies. But you can start to look at those companies not as gatekeepers but rather as *maximizers*. They might help you maximize your writing skills, or maximize your marketing efforts, or maximize your revenue. But that's it. The gate is gone.

Look at what we have now: self-publishing, blogging, app stores, YouTube, and crowdfunding. There are so many ways to share your work with the world. The platforms are there.

So what's the problem? You tell me. Have you published a book or an article, produced a video game, released a TV show or movie, or published a board game? Have you done the thing you've always wanted to do? Think about those lifelong dreams you keep putting off for tomorrow.

The problem is that *you are your own gatekeeper.* You might have a dream project, but *you haven't created it yet.*

We're living in an exciting time. I hope you realize how amazing it is that you are your own gatekeeper. I also hope, though, that if you have something awesome to share with the world, you don't wait too long. You owe that to yourself.

I waited until I was twenty-seven to write my first blog entry. I waited until I was thirty to write my first novel. And I waited until I was thirty-two to publish my first board game. I hope you don't take nearly as long as I did to experience the joy of creating and sharing something you love.

125 Crowdfunding Lessons in 125 Sentences

My crowdfunding blog has grown from humble roots – a few core concepts – to a bloated 150+ blog entries detailing how to create, run, and deliver a successful crowdfunding campaign. If you like this book and want to start walking down the path to becoming a crowdfunder, I highly recommend reading every entry on my blog.

I say that not because I get anything out of it—the blog is free for you, free of banner ads and endorsements and all that crap—but rather because everything I write is there for the sole purpose of helping you become a better crowdfunder. The details and the reasons behind those details are important.

I'm preface this list with that point because what you'll find below are the key takeaways from the first 137 crowdfunding lessons on my blog. They're each just one or two sentences, so if they leave you wanting to know more, all you have to do is go to my blog.[1] They're all there.

The lessons that follow are in chronological order from start to finish, not the order in which I wrote them. That is, no. 1 is something you should start thinking about six to twelve months before you launch your project, and no. 125 is something related to the process well after your campaign ends. The number in parentheses is the number of the lesson (a few lessons don't have numbers). I've separated the lessons into three big time periods: before your campaign, during it, and what you do afterward.

Before You Launch the Project

1. **The Shortcut to Crowdfunding Success** (#110)   There are creators who get lucky without putting in much time or effort, but they're not the norm. Put yourself in a position to succeed by forming relationships and building a fan base well in advance of launching your campaign.

2. **Preventing a Dud** (#86)   Does the idea of running a business sound fun to you? If not, you may want to consider a different path from crowdfunding because every creator is a business owner by default, whether you like it or not.

3. **Write a Blog** (#52)   Writing a blog will contribute three key assets to your future crowdfunding campaign: it will teach you how to connect with people online, it will help you develop a readership and a fan base (with good luck), and it will give you a wealth of content to share.

4. **Starting and Submitting Your Project Page** (#1)   It's never too early to start working on your project page. If you want to run a crowdfunding campaign, this is one of the first things you can do to motivate yourself.

5. **How to Give and Take Tough-Love Feedback** (#123)   When you ask for feedback on your project's preview page well before the launch—from people you know and from complete strangers—ask a few specific questions about aspects of the project you're truly open to changing based on the input you receive.

6. **Minimum Viable Product** (#105)   Don't spend years behind closed doors perfecting your product—instead, get the rough version in people's hands as soon as possible so that you can see firsthand what works and what doesn't.

7. **Back Other Projects** (#2)   If you're going to build a community leading up to a crowdfunding campaign, start by backing other projects involved in that community.

8. **How to Effectively Research Other Projects** (#56)   By backing other projects (within and outside your project category) and following them closely throughout the campaign, you will learn firsthand how to run a project, especially in terms of backer communication and engagement.

9. **Megaprojects and You** (#112)   Many of the most successful crowdfunding projects do well despite key flaws that you should not replicate on your project. When looking at megaprojects, make sure to dig under the surface to get the true story on what made them so successful.

10. **The Top Ten Ways to Survive and Thrive on Online Forums** (#94) Find the place online where people go to talk about the category your product is related to. Spend time there every day participating in the community, not promoting yourself or your future project.

11 **Art and Design** (#3)   Every campaign needs at least a few pieces of very attractive, high-quality art, even if part of the reason you're crowdfunding is to raise money for art. Pay for a great artist—be sure to get a few disinterested opinions when selecting an artist to ensure that you're not blinded by your own biases.

12. **Card Frames** (#85)   Great graphic design can help people overlook mediocre art. It's worth every cent—pay for a professional to handle your graphic design.

13. **Accounting and Finances** (#4)   Project creators must pay income tax on crowdfunding revenue, so to make your life

a lot easier when it comes to tax season, open checking and PayPal accounts right now solely for your company. By using the accrual method of accounting, you will pay taxes only in the year when you deliver the project rewards.

14. **The Four Legal Issues Every Creator Should Know** (#114)   By forming some kind of official entity for your business (usually an LLC or a corporation), you protect your personal assets in case your company gets sued or goes bankrupt, and it makes it easier to sell or transfer your business in the long run if such an opportunity should present itself.

15. **Partnership** (#45)   Finding a partner for your business can help balance out your weaknesses, give you a person with whom to brainstorm regularly, and allow you to share the heavy workload.

16. **The Value of Ambassadors**   Form a team of supporters who can help represent you in a variety of places (around the world), times (when you're sleeping), and ways (areas beyond your expertise). Reward them with special discounts, opportunities, and insider knowledge.

17. **Connecting with Bloggers** (#5)   Forge relationships with bloggers, podcasters, and other content creators well in advance of your project launch, and then offer them some type of invaluable content for their platform during the campaign (a guest post, interview, and so on).

18. **Creating Prototypes for Third-Party Reviewers** (#78)   When you create any type of prototype to send to third-party reviewers before the campaign, use all resources available to make the prototype functional and visually attractive (especially for reviewers who include visual elements such as photos or video).

19. **Help Them First** (#74)   The secret to getting strangers to
    help you—whether it's to proofread your project page, share
    your project, blog about your product, and what not—is to
    help them first.

20. **Pick the Right Name** (#129)   When selecting the name for
    your project, make sure it's not trademarked and find a
    name that is search friendly and easy to spell.

21. **The Project Video** (#6)   Your main project video should be no
    longer than two minutes, convey your excitement and pas-
    sion for the project, explain what the product is, and express
    what makes the product unique and interesting.

22. **The Funding Goal** (#7)   Your funding goal should be the
    minimum amount of money you need to make the project a
    reality, minus the amount of money you're personally willing
    to invest in it, plus some built-in wiggle room for risk and
    unforeseen expenses.

23. **The Three Funding Scenarios You Must Plan For** (#117)   Every
    crowdfunder should consider these funding scenarios in
    terms of asset management, campaign execution, manufac-
    turing, and shipping: (1) you don't reach your funding goal;
    (2) you barely reach your funding goal; and (3) you wildly
    surpass your funding goal.

24. **Reward Levels** (#8)   Launch your project with five to seven
    reward levels ($1, core reward, core reward + bonus, and a
    few limited high-level rewards), each succinctly worded (no
    more than eight lines of text each); you can add a few more
    reward levels during the project if you need to.

25. **Why Every Project Should Have a $1 Reward Level** (#113)   Your
    project should have a fun, thematic $1 reward level
    because this gives backers a way to follow the project in an

inexpensive, noncommittal way so that you have the opportunity to engage them through comments and project
updates. Many $1 reward backers will eventually upgrade to
the core reward level.

26. **Stay Focused or Lose Backers** (#63)   Stay focused on what
you're raising money for through the wording on your project page; stay focused on whom you're creating it for by identifying and reaching out to your target audience; stay focused
on what you're trying to deliver to backers by eliminating
ancillary add-ons and reward levels.

27. **There Is No Perfect Pickle** (#103)   Leading up to the campaign, spend a significant amount of time brainstorming
various rewards for different types of people and surveying
people about those ideas until you hone the rewards into the
five to seven rewards you'll present to backers on launch day.

28. **Early-Bird Pledge Levels** (#62)   The purpose of early birds
is to cajole backers into backing now instead of backing
later. There are better ways to do this, like offering limited
reward levels (not the core reward), offering a great product
on a great project page, offering a fair price to everyone, and
reaching out to friends and family (if this is your first project). Early birds have the negative effect of creating a system
of winners and losers among backers, all of whom are trying
to support the creation of something that doesn't yet exist.

29. **The Premium Option** (#54)   The premium option is a highly
compelling reward level that costs slightly more than the
core reward level but offers a special version of the product
to backers.

30. **Should You Offer Multiple Copies of Your Product at a Reduced
Bundled Price?** (#111)   Bundled pricing at a slight discount

(that is, if a product is listed as a $29 reward, create a separate reward offering two for $55 or three for $79) works because it gives backers a good deal, it encourages backers to share the project with their friends (to buy in together), it's easier for backers who want multiple copies for themselves, and it allows international backers to spread out the high shipping cost among multiple people.

31. **How to Get US Backers If You're Running a Non-US-Based Crowdfunding Campaign (#65)**   US backers are deterred by foreign currency conversion, so make it easy for them by listing the USD price in the reward levels and on the project page.

32. **The Magic of Automatic Currency Conversion (#116)**   As you're creating your reward level prices, use a currency converter to view the project through the eyes of backers in other countries.

33. **The Myth of MSRP (#59)**   Determine your product's MSRP by looking at other similar products, and list the MSRP in your reward levels so that backers know they're getting a discount for pledging early instead of waiting for the retail version.

34. **It's Not the Job of the Crowdfunding Site to Give You Backers (#57)**   Every aspect of your project should be created with the intent of attracting and engaging backers and giving them something awesome for a fair price—your project should be backer focused, not focused on the slim chance that the crowdfunding site will feature your project (which will give you a little boost at best).

35. **Timing and Length (#9)**   Launch your campaign around 10:00 a.m. EST on any day but Saturday, and end the

campaign about a month later (less if you're a repeat creator) on or soon after a bimonthly payday, any day but Friday, around 10:00 p.m. EST.

36. **Seasonal Timing** (#109)   If your product is on people's minds or solves a problem in a particular season, run the campaign during that season (even though the product won't be delivered for months later).

37. **Coordinating Staggered Launch and End Dates** (#84)   Try to be aware of other crowdfunded products in your category, and don't launch on the same day as a similar product. For tabletop game products, I host a spreadsheet where you can stake an unofficial claim on a certain day (and see when other similar games are launching or ending).

38. **The Taste Test** (#10)   If this applies to your product, make a free "lite" version of your product available on the project page (and in advance of launching) for anyone to download and test out. This will increase engagement, trust, pledges, and the quality of the product itself.

39. **The Art of Pitching** (#73)   The more you're able to make your potential backers feel like collaborators, the more likely they are to back your project.

40. **The Ten Reasons I'll Back a Crowdfunding Project** (#10)   Consider the following from the backer perspective when creating your project page: art, graphic design, value, engagement, uniqueness, competence, passion, generosity, quality, and pliability.

41. **Give Credit Where Credit Is Due . . . Including to Yourself** (#96)   It feels good to be credited, so as often as possible, credit specific people who make an impact on your project in

specific ways: partners, ambassadors, artists, bloggers, and most importantly, backers.

42. **Stretch Goals** (#11)   Plan out stretch goals in advance of the project and feature a few on the project page on launch day (save the full reveal until after the original burst of funding). Stretch goals should be included with all core rewards to encourage backers to share the project by adding real value to the product without negatively affecting the budget or schedule.

43. **Include at Least One Must-Have Component** (#75)   For projects with multiple components of varying degrees of quality, feature photographs of one particularly attractive component on the project page from day 1 (either as part of the product or as one of the first stretch goals).

44. **Exclusive Content** (#60)   Instead of offering exclusive content for the project to induce "fear of missing out," give backers special content as part of the core rewards and make this content available separate from the core product only after the project for an additional cost.

45. **Shipping** (#12)   Find shipping solutions (that is, fulfillment companies) that work best for backers around the world—don't apply a one-size-fits-all strategy, because shipping rates vary widely depending on the destination.

46. **This Project Is EU Friendly** (#47)   The best way to attract backers to your project who are from the EU (to avoid customs, taxes, and other fees) is to find a fulfillment company in Europe that will send out individual rewards to backers there.

47. **Explaining Why You Need the Funds** (#13)   Tell backers in simple terms the costs you've already covered versus what you need the funds for.

48. **How to Kick It Forward without Kicking It Forward** (#44)   The single best way to show backers that you are an active, generous, and experienced member of the greater crowdfunding community is to back a lot of projects.

49. **The Value of Add-Ons** (#14)   Limit add-ons to one or two items, preferably with bar codes or included in the box of your core product under a special SKU.

50. **Anatomy of a Great Project Page** (#39)   Keep text on your project page succinct and in list form when possible, feature the best art and attractive graphic design, and limit reward levels (which should be heavily proofread for clarity) to eight or fewer lines.

51. **The Value of Agonizing over Your Project Page**   Start working on your project page two months before launch, and make at least one improvement to it every day.

52. **The Psychological Benefit of Showing Your Face** (#64)   Make a project personal and increase backer empathy by showing your face in the video, your profile photo, and occasional project updates.

53. **The Psychological Benefits of Framing Your Project's Potential** (#66)   Include a line on the project page that does not boast or tell backers how they should feel, but rather frames the product's potential: "[your product] could be the next [highly acclaimed product]."

54. **The Psychological Benefits of Ending Price Points with the Number 9** (#92)   By having the most important reward levels feature pledge prices that end with the number 9, studies indicate that you will increase the number of pledges for those rewards by 24 percent (when compared with other ending digits).

55. **Risks and Challenges** (#125)   If you are using Kickstarter, be open, transparent, and vulnerable in the mandatory "Risks and Challenges" section, while instilling confidence in backers that you've properly budgeted and researched every step of the product-creation process. This may not be mandatory on other crowdfunding platforms, but including a section like this instills confidence in backers.

56. **The One-Week Checklist** (#104)   Create a checklist for the final week leading up to your project launch (see the full example later in this book).

57. **How to Get Google to Rank Your Website Higher Than Your Project Page** (#89)   To ensure that postcampaign traffic goes to your website and not the stagnant project page, create and share a 302 redirect link the sends potential backers seamlessly through your website to the project page before and during the campaign. Some crowdfunding platforms (like Kickstarter) now offer a way to make subtle changes to the landing page to help redirect people to more current information.

58. **Finishing Touches: FAQ and Preview** (#15)   While sharing your project preview page on social media and with friends to get feedback on it, gather questions and answer them in writing in preparation for filling out the project FAQ on launch day (you can't post an FAQ on the project page in advance).

59. **Press Releases** (#43)   A week before launch, send an informative press release to the media relevant to your project that includes what the product is and what's special about it, when the project will launch, social media links to you, and the project preview link.

60. **The Secrets to Making Your Tabletop Game Crowdfunding Project Appealing to Retailers**   Send retailers a special notice about your project one week before launch. Highlight the project, offer a retailer-only ten-unit package available at 50 percent off MSRP during the campaign, and send the product to these retailers before general distribution. Retailers also love special promo items.

61. **Setting and Achieving Goals** (#23)   Before launching your project, write down a specific goal to pursue (record a podcast, connect with a specific blogger, and so on) or announcement to make for every day of the campaign.

62. **You Don't Need to Launch Today** (#68)   Even if you've been telling people that you're going to launch on a certain day, if the project isn't 100 percent ready and optimized for success, you don't need to launch today.

During the Project

63. **Launch Day** (#16)   Take the day off work and spend launch day sending personal messages to friends and family (if it's your first project), chatting with backers in the comments section, and sending personal thank-you messages to every backer.

64. **How to Include People Who Don't Know What Crowdfunding Is** (#120)   Creators should explain crowdfunding in simple terms to those who are new to the concept. Also, to make actions such as adding funds to a pledge for an add-on or changing a reward selection easier for all backers to understand, be sure to outline specific steps on the project page and in updates.

65. **Momentum Breeds Success** (#101)   The first few days of a campaign are incredibly important because early momentum significantly increases both the *perception* and the *mathematical odds* that the project will successfully fund.

66. **Treat Your Backers As Individuals, Not Numbers** (#17)   As easy as it is to view backers in sums and totals, the magic of crowdfunding is that you have the opportunity to form a personal connection with each and every backer. By sending individualized thank-you messages to backers, you create an opportunity for that relationship to grow in a way that could turn any one-time backer into a lifelong fan, supporter, and even friend.

67. **People Are More Compelling Than Numbers** (#71)   Backers respond better and with more empathy to creators who treat them as individuals instead of wallets—don't continually ask backers to pledge more, share more, and do more. It's already enough that they're a backer. Now get to know them.

68. **Cancellations** (#38 and #79)   The ability of backers to cancel their pledge during the campaign is part of what makes certain crowdfunding platforms great. No one is bound by their pledge during the campaign, so backers feel comfortable pledging now and pulling out later if needed. It's tough not to take cancellations personally, so I recommend ignoring them altogether by using your e-mail client to filter out cancellation alerts before you see them. Rather than focus on the 5 percent of people who changed their mind about your project, focus on the 95 percent who have decided to stick with you.

69. **Passion Is Contagious** (#102)   Create a foundation for contagious passion about your project by exuding joy in updates

and comments, inspiring confidence through the structure of the project page, showing conviction regarding your product's uniqueness, telling a great story about how you came up with the idea and the decisions that go on behind the scenes, and connecting with backers about your shared passions that intersect with the project.

70. **Creation Is Leadership** (#98)   Have a clear vision to connect with people who believe the same thing you do, make backers feel safe through sacrifice and respect, and communicate your expectations clearly to your partners.

71. **Project Updates** (#18)   Every two to three days during a campaign, post project updates that are relevant, insightful, important, and urgent—the purpose is to maintain the same level of excitement backers experienced when they first discovered and backed your project.

72. **The Best Opening Lines for Project Updates and Backer E-mails** (#115)   Begin each update or group message (you can send a message to all backers of a specific reward) as though you're talking to one person ("Hi!"), not a group of people ("Hey everyone!")—thus each backer can feel like you're writing specifically to that backer.

73. **Updating Previous Projects**   If you want to alert previous backers to your latest campaign, write project updates specifically for each of those campaigns, connecting the backers' passion for the original project to the current one.

74. **Backer-Only Project Updates** (#99)   You have the ability to make project updates available only to backers, but don't do it. These updates close off information to potential backers, and they don't allow members of group buys to follow the project the way they'd like to.

75. **What You Should Do for Thirty Minutes after Posting a Project Update** (#90)   It's really important to post project updates at times when you're available to respond to questions and comments right away. Also, Kickstarter allows creators to edit the text of an update within the first thirty minutes after posting it in case a backer points out an embarrassing or confusing typo.

76. **Flexibility, Filtering, and Responding to Feedback** (#20) Respect backers and encourage participation by responding to their ideas and comments, but stay true to your vision, your budget, and your schedule when deciding which of those ideas to pursue.

77. **How to Say No** (#107)   One gentle way to say no when a backer proposes an idea is to ask that backer to outline, step by step, exactly how this request could become reality. Often, by trying to explain the idea, the backer realizes that the idea won't work. And sometimes the backer might stumble on a solution you hadn't considered, giving you an opportunity to say yes!

78. **Kicktraq** (#21)   Look at Kicktraq, a site with a web-browser extension that compiles data from Kickstarter to estimate your project's final funding total, starting on day 9 (any earlier and you'll have delusions of grandeur). Correlate this data to the different types of outreach you do during the project to identify what works and what doesn't.

79. **The Money-Back Guarantee and Trust** (#22)   By offering a money-back guarantee, you establish trust and accountability with backers and reduce the barrier to entry ("If you don't like it, you can return it within a month of receiving it for a full refund").

80. **Backer Engagement** (#24)   Make sure that the product is 90–95 percent complete, and ask backers for input on the final 5–10 percent. This gives backers a sense of ownership.

81. **The Ten Elements of Great Customer Service for a Creator** (#72) Customers aren't always right, but they're always respected. Be responsive, compassionate, attentive, fair, proactive, transparent, tactful, human, humble, and culpable.

82. **It's Okay to Say No** (#48)   Be honest with backers about what you can or cannot do for them, especially when a backer asks for an individual, special favor or exception (that's a completely appropriate time to say no).

83. **Your Target Audience Is Not "Everyone"** (#46)   Figure out the core audience for your product and focus the majority of your time, effort, and advertising dollars on that audience.

84. **How to Manage Toxic Backers** (#58)   When a backer creates a negative, unwelcoming environment through his or her comments, reply as positively as possible in public, and message the backer in private to try to get to the heart of the toxicity.

85. **Give Each Backer a Voice** (#127)   To encourage backers to be a part of your project's community, whenever a backer shares an idea in comments, recognize the backer's creativity, explain why you can or cannot implement the idea, and every now and then, make sure to act on at least a minor suggestion to show backers that their ideas are valued.

86. **How to Create Community through Conversation on Kickstarter** (#80)   When moderating crowdfunding comments, *encourage* comments and questions about the project, product, and each backer's connection to the campaign, but *discourage* conversation about other projects, truly off-topic

conversations that might discourage other backers from participating, and minute-by-minute posts about project statistics.

87. **Don't Copy and Paste** (#106)   When you copy and paste individual or group messages to backers, you eliminate the opportunity to connect with each backer. Instead, view that backer as an individual and open a genuine line of communication with him or her.

88. **How to Have Fun with Your Backers** (#88)   Self-deprecating humor and a playful spirit can make running a project a lot of fun for you (and for backers) as long as your goofy comments don't confuse backers out of context.

89. **The Three Secrets to Marketing** (#100)   Stop promoting your project and start making friends.

90. **The Five Love Languages of Crowdfunding** (#122)   Each backer feels valued and derives value in a unique way that is often very different from how you do. By paying attention to the way different backers interact with the project, you can expand the scope of the project well beyond what it would be if you focused only on what *you* want out of a crowdfunding campaign.

91. **Reddit** (#25)   As one of the biggest and most active websites on the Internet, Reddit can draw a lot of attention to your project. Ideally, someone else will start a conversation about your project on Reddit, and you can join in the conversation as a participant, *not* to promote your campaign.

92. **Paid Advertising and How Backers Find Your Project** (#26)   A small amount of paid advertising focused on your core audience can provide a significant boost to your project. Aim to do this during the mid-campaign slump.

93. **My Thoughts on Campaign Boosting Services** (#91)   Don't use them. Services that guarantee to send a certain number of backers your way aren't focused on your primary audience and are a poor use of your budget.

94. **Bloggers, Podcasters, and Reviewers** (#27)   As you look to expand your reach during the project, contact blogs you enjoy reading (it's fine if you just recently discovered them), tell them why you like them, and offer them something of value (interview, guest post, prototype to review).

95. **Social Networks** (#28)   You will lose the respect and attention of your Facebook and Twitter followers if you spam them with pleas to back your project. Instead, post sparingly about the project (and in a way that adds value to the reader's day, perhaps through humor), and once or twice during a project, ask backers to share the project with exactly *one* person.

96. **Overestimating and Underestimating Your Tribe** (#96)   While it's often helpful to build up a fan base before launching a crowdfunding project, if that fan base is only tangentially connected to the product, very few of them will become backers.

97. **Hometown Press and Local Media** (#29)   If both you and your project have a direct connection to a specific locality, pursue as much local press as possible. Otherwise, pursuing media attention rarely has much of an impact, and your time could be better spent on your primary audience.

98. **The Matching Pledge** (#30)   If you have a backer who wants to give a large sum of money, see whether the backer would agree to match all pledges made on a certain day during the mid-project slump, which can ignite a flurry of pledges and shares.

99. **Cross Promotion between Projects** (#51)   If there is another project that (a) hasn't solicited your cross promotion, (b) you really believe in or have a strong connection to, and (c) would really benefit and excite your specific backers, then it's worth sharing it with your backers. Then, after you do so, reach out to the other project creator and say, "Hey, I love what you're doing so much that I shared it in this project update. Thanks for being awesome!" There's no request, no obligation for them to return the favor. That's the only way for a mention of another project to be genuine instead of a cross-promotion marketing gimmick that will annoy backers.

100. **Contests** (#82)   Kickstarter does not allow any type of contest or lottery to be mentioned on the project page, as rewards, or in updates. This may vary on other platforms. However, running contests through social media is a fun way to engage backers.

101. **Microgoals** (#31)   Throughout the project, present backers with small goals (for example, if you have 239 backers, get to 250 by the end of the day) to give them an achievable reason to act now.

102. **The Top Ten Ways to Address the Mid-campaign Slump** (#95)
     Focus inwardly by talking to existing backers about ways to make the project as good as it can possibly be, and then (and only then) shift part of your attention outwardly through personal appeals to friends and family to back at the $1 level, offers of content to bloggers and podcasters, and the creation of targeted advertising.

103. **To Cancel or to Finish** (#49)   If your project has earned less than 33 percent of the funding goal by day 14, this is a sign

that there is either something wrong with the project or
there isn't enough demand for the product, and I recommend canceling the project.

104. **How to Reboot an Unsuccessful Project** (#50)   Gather feedback from backers (and people who didn't back the original
campaign if you have access to them) about why the original
campaign didn't work, refine the project, then reboot within
four months of the original project's launch date (ideally
with a lower funding goal, a slightly lower core reward price,
and a reduction of any confusing elements present on the
original project).

105. **The Final Week** (#32)   Create a frenzy surrounding your project through exciting project updates every couple of days,
new or reorganized stretch goals, and calls to action for backers to share the project.

106. **Project Creep** (#89)   It's the project creator's responsibility
to maintain the integrity of the campaign itself (by limiting
the number of polls, calls to action, and project updates)
and to keep the project within the original scope so that the
product can be manufactured successfully and delivered on
schedule.

107. **The Final Sixty Hours** (#108)   Unlike nonbackers who
pressed the Remind Me button, backers do not receive an
automated reminder during the final few days of a project. Many backers appreciate a reminder so that they can be
sure their reward level is correct and that they've included
any add-ons that may not have existed at the time of their
original pledge. So send group messages to backers in each
reward level to thank them for their pledge, inform them

that the project is ending soon, and that there are some things available now on the project that weren't available before. Teach them how to change their pledge if that's what they want to do, and end by saying their pledge is great just the way it is.

108. **The Final Forty-Eight Hours** (#33)   To maximize the potential of your project during the final forty-eight hours, be sure that the project page is restructured in a way that presents the best possible pitch for what the project is now (including any unlocked stretch goals and new add-ons) to people who return to the project through the crowdfunding platform's automated "Remind Me" e-mail.

109. **The Final Hour** (#34)   You can't edit the project page after the campaign ends, so during the final hour be sure to place at the top of the project page a prominent link to your website for people to click on if they discover the project after time runs out.

110. **Platform Limitations and How to Work around Them** (#35)   For backers who are unable to place a pledge through the crowdfunding platform's payment system, paste a link to PayPal in the FAQ.

After the Project Ends

111. **Don't Quit Your Day Job** (#81)   Even if you raise a lot of money through crowdfunding, don't quit your day job when those funds arrive in your bank account. Wait until you've actually produced and delivered the product to backers.

112. **Visioning** (#121)   Build toward a specific future by hosting a small "visioning day" (or evening) at which you brainstorm

thoughts about what your company is today, what it could be tomorrow, and how to get there.

113. **For Better or for Worse** (#36)   When sending out postproject updates, bad news is better than no news. Keep backers consistently informed and engaged by offering transparent and interesting reports about the development, production, and shipping processes.

114. **Postcampaign Communication** (#61)   Offer backers a variety of ways to stay in touch after the campaign, based on their personal preferences: project updates, e-newsletter, blog, Facebook, and Twitter are examples.

115. **If You Manufacture in China, Account for Chinese Holidays** (#124)   Keep a close eye on deadlines or scheduling promises made for early February and early October because Chinese production and communication will be nearly nonexistent during those times.

116. **Conventions and Face Time** (#37)   Many backers who get to know you through crowdfunding will be excited to meet you in person, and conventions are a great place for those next-level interactions.

117. **Should You Offer the Exclusive Version of Your Product after the Campaign?** (#40)   The answer is no, unless you want to lose the loyalty and trust of many backers.

118. **How to Sell the Retail Version of Your Product Online Postcampaign** (#70)   Build a store into your website using PayPal, ShopLocket, Shopify, WooCommerce, Celery, or another e-commerce platform, or sell through platforms such as Amazon.com, Outgrow.me, and Stiqblox.

119. **Starting and Sustaining a Crowdfunding-Driven Business** (#55) Have fun. Not every task you do will be fun, but if you're not having fun, even a financially successful business won't be sustainable.

120. **Etiquette in the Public Eye** (#41)   Becoming a crowdfunder significantly raises your public exposure. Everything you say on social media is now part of your brand. When expressing your opinions, praise publicly and criticize privately.

121. **The Backer Survey** (#42)   Crowdfunding platforms allows creators to send out a postproject survey to backers at each reward level. Send the survey within a few weeks after the project ends, as many backers will take a long time to reply, and you may need to send products directly from your manufacturer to specific regions around the world. Make sure to request an address where a person can personally receive the shipment during the day (such as a work address).

122. **Pledge Managers**   In a poll on my blog, of backers who had a preference, 64 percent preferred to use the crowdfunding platform's built-in survey software instead of third-party pledge managers.

123. **The Address Update E-mail** (#59)   About ten days to two weeks before you expect the products to be delivered to backers, send a mass e-mail requesting address updates for any backers who have moved since they filled out the original backer survey.

124. **Delivering on Time** (#97)   Do everything in your power to deliver the product by the estimated delivery date, but don't sacrifice quality. Keep backers informed throughout the process by using public project updates.

125. **Release with a Boom, Not a Whimper** (#119)   Backers will have the best experience when they finally receive their rewards if they feel like "everyone" is using the product as soon as it arrives. Do things to breed perceived popularity by writing backer updates with engaging questions, posting photos online (and asking backers to post photos), and sending copies to reviewers.

The One-Week Checklist

Whenever I'm getting ready to launch a new project, I create a lengthy to-do list. It usually starts about two months before the launch day and ends a week or so after the project completion date. The most crucial period of time, however, is the week leading up to launch. That's crunch time.

This isn't an exact science; if you do these things in a different order or over two weeks instead of one week, that's fine. Every project is different.

Seven Days before Launch

- Update the front page of your blog to reflect the upcoming campaign.

- Update your Facebook page banner with a representative image for the project.

- Submit your project for approval if needed (you can do this long before you plan to launch, but the reminder is here in case you haven't already done so).

Six Days before Launch

- Write the FAQ so that you can post it as soon as you launch.

- Send the project preview link to a small group of trusted advisors and partners.

Five Days before Launch

- Read through "125 Crowdfunding Lessons in 125 Sentences," earlier in this book, as a refresher.

- Design any ads you plan to post during the campaign, and send them to the websites where they'll be displayed.

- If you plan to run any ongoing polls or surveys during your campaign, create a dedicated page on your blog to host those surveys.

Four Days before Launch

- Design project avatars for backers to use as their profile photos during the campaign.

- Send the project preview link to a larger group of people whose opinions you respect. For Stonemaier Games, this means our ambassadors. The Kickstarter Best Practices and Lessons Learned Facebook group is a great place to get blunt, honest feedback (just make sure you go here *before* the project launches and for the purpose of getting feedback, not to promote your project).

- Prepare a few other people to help you with comment moderation and community building during the project.

Three Days before Launch

- Double-check with your manufacturer to be sure they're ready for any questions that might arise during the campaign. Many backers will have suggestions about things to add or change, so you'll need a quick response from your manufacturer.

- If you're working with a business partner, have a chat to make sure that expectations and responsibilities for running the project are clearly understood.

- Finalize the project video (you should have already done this).

Two Days before Launch

- Be sure that all photos and links on the project page are up to date.

- Send out a press release with key information and project preview link.

- Send out a sneak preview to retailers, highlighting the benefits for them to back the project

One Day before Launch

- Do one final review of your project page, *especially* the elements you can't edit after you launch: reward levels, funding goal, and project duration.

- If you have any ancillary products on your website, put them on sale.

- Prepare your launch notification e-newsletter.

- Disable the Kicktraq extension on your web browser. Kicktraq is a website that creates projections for Kickstarter campaigns based on a monumental amount of data. It isn't particularly accurate until day 9 of the campaign because of the jump in funding early on that skews the projection.

- Adjust your e-mail settings to filter out cancellation notification e-mails. Cancellation e-mails will crush your spirit even if your project is going well—you're better off focusing your energy on the backers who stick with you, not the 5 percent who will back the project and cancel before the project ends.

First Ten Minutes after Launching

- Send out the launch notification e-newsletter.
- Copy and paste the FAQ you've written onto the project page.
- Post the crowdfunding widget on your website.
- Mention the project launch on relevant third-party websites where you're already engaged in the community.
- Update the Shop Now button on your Facebook page to take people to the project page.

Recommended Reading

Kickstarter Lessons blog (Jamey Stegmaier)   This is my ever-growing list of articles about how to be a better crowdfunder.
www.kickstarterlessons.com

Funding the Dream Podcast (Richard Bliss)   This is a fantastic twenty-minute podcast with more than 240 episodes, most of them interviews with creators about specific aspects of crowdfunding.
www.buzzsprout.com/4646/

jamesmathe.com (James Mathe)   James is a successful creator who shares his insights in long, list-based entries that are chock full of information.
www.jamesmathe.com

Kicktraq (Adam Clark)   Kicktraq is known for its hotlist and projection algorithms, but it also features a wealth of must-read crowdfunding articles.
www.kicktraq.com

Genius Games (John Coveyou)   If you love statistics, you'll love this website. John takes a data-driven approach to evaluating what works and doesn't work on crowdfunding.
www.gotgeniusgames.com/blogs/

Kickstarter Best Practices Facebook Group   This is one of the best resources for project creators. The group features a ton of members who want to make crowdfunding better. If you ask for advice here, be sure you truly are open to it.
www.facebook.com/groups/KickstarterBestPractices/

ComixTribe (Tyler James)   Tyler and his cohorts write about a lot of topics, but every now and then they publish some of the best articles on crowdfunding.
http://www.comixtribe.com/tag/kickstarter/

SunTzuGames (Emil Larsen)   Emil offers one of the few YouTube channels specifically geared toward helping project creators.
www.suntzugames.com/kickstarter-study

CrowdCrux (Salvador Briggman)   CrowdCrux is a fantastic resource for learning about how to be a more effective creator. I appreciate that Salvador shares my philosophies on how crowdfunding is more about building community than raising money.

www.crowdcrux.com

Crowdfunding Dojo   I like sites that use specific projects to teach other creators, and Crowdfunding Dojo does a great job of that.

www.crowdfundingdojo.com

Crowdsourcing.org   This site is a little different from the others—it's like the *Financial Times* for crowdfunding.

www.crowdsourcing.org

Gate Keeper Games (John Wrot)   John lends his Kickstarter and Indiegogo experience—as well as his background as an accountant—to this detailed series.

www.gatekeepergaming.com/kickstarter-advice-columns

The following chart lists all crowdfunding projects mentioned in this book. To learn more about these projects, search Kickstarter for the project name (there are also a few projects from Indiegogo and Patreon).

Project Name/Creator Name	Funding Total	Backer Total	Core Reward Price	Project Length (days)	Launch Date (mm/yy)
1 Second Everyday App *Cesar Kuriyama*	$56,959	11,281	$1	30	11/12
Alien Frontiers *Clever Mojo Games*	$14,885	228	$50	60	04/10
The Beer Hammer *Luke Brown*	$16,402	349	$30	30	10/14
Between Two Cities *Jamey Stegmaier*	$221,265	5,287	$29	20	02/15
Bluebird Man *Wild Lens Inc.*	$17,241	207	$20	30	06/13
Boom or Doom! Kickstarter Adventures in the Tabletop World *Alan Gerding & Sean McCoy*	$4,550	113	$10	30	08/13
Burning Suns *Emil Larsen*	$142,985	1,313	$88	45	08/13
Coin Age *Tasty Minstrel Games*	$65,195	9,055	$3	11	12/13
The Coolest cooler (original) *Ryan Grepper*	$102,188	279	$185	30	11/13
The Coolest cooler (reboot) *Ryan Grepper*	$13.2 million	62,642	$185	52	07/14
The Cosmonaut *Studio Neat*	$134,236	6,192	$25	23	03/11
The Doom That Came to Atlantic City *Erik Chevalier*	$122,874	1,246	$75	30	05/12
Dungeon Roll *Tasty Minstrel Games*	$250,070	10,877	$15	21	02/13
Eminent Domain *Tasty Minstrel Games*	$48,378	699	$35	29	10/10

Project Name/Creator Name	Funding Total	Backer Total	Core Reward Price	Project Length (days)	Launch Date (mm/yy)
Exploding Kittens *Matthew Inman, Elan Lee, and Shane Small*	In progress	In progress	$35	30	01/15
Euphoria: Build a Better Dystopia *Jamey Stegmaier*	$309,495	4,765	$49	28	05/13
Home Aquaponics Kit *Nikhil Arora and Alex Velez*	$248,873	4,097	$50	30	11/12
The Icarus Deception *Seth Godin*	$287,342	4,242	$62	29	06/12
The King's Armory (original) *John Wrot!*	$25,279	362	$49	40	07/13
The King's Armory (art) — Indiegogo *John Wrot!*	$3,774	66	$65	29	09/13
The King's Armory (reboot) *John Wrot!*	$90,389	815	$50	30	10/13
Lanterns: The Harvest Festival *Foxtrot Games*	$33,523	1,213	$24	29	10/14
Lift Off! *Eduardo Baraf*	$50,462	1,014	$39	28	07/14
Linkage *John Coveyou*	$12,055	616	$14	35	04/14
Neat Ice Kit *Studio Neat*	$155,519	2,274	$50	30	08/13
Otters! *Michael Iachini*	$5,321	246	$12	28	01/14
Pebble *Eric Migicovsky*	$10.2 million	68,929	$115	37	04/12
Pleasant Dreams: A Card Game of Nightmares *Aerjen Tamminga*	$11,327	604	$15	33	03/14
Propel Two Authors Towards the Future of Publishing (Blank Slate Press) *Jamey Stegmaier*	$305	17	$10	30	06/11
Quinn Popcorn *Kristy and Coulter Lewis*	$27,880	755	$15	30	07/11

Project Name/Creator Name	Funding Total	Backer Total	Core Reward Price	Project Length (days)	Launch Date (mm/yy)
Reading Rainbow *LeVar Burton*	$5.4 million	105,857	$25	35	05/14
Rise! *Crash Games*	$17,518	410	$20	60	11/11
Robin Writes a Book *Robin Sloan*	$13,942	570	$11	67	08/09
The Secret Around-the-World Adventures of Owney the Postal Dog *David Montgomery & Marcelo Vital*	$10,340	142	$20	31	10/12
The Secret Cabal Gaming Podcast (Patreon) *SCGP*	$460.15/episode	193	$1	N/A	12/14
Soberdough *Veronica and Jordan Hawbaker*	$10,074	254	$13	37	06/13
Stonemaier Games Treasure Chest *Jamey Stegmaier*	$181,157	3,221	$33	17	06/14
Tex Murphy—Project Fedora *Chris Jones and Aaron Conners*	$598,104	6,963	$15	32	05/12
Three New Treasure Chests *Stonemaier Games*	$207,817	2,184	$35	16	04/15
Tiny Epic Galaxies *Michael Coe*	$411,693	12,458	$16	30	01/15
TKMB: Precision Machined *Brad Martin*	$42,403	678	$55	40	10/13
Torn Armor *Natalya Alyssa Faden*	$67,742	561	$150	32	03/13
Trickerion *Mindclash Games*	$285,309	4,330	$49	30	01/15
Tuscany *Jamey Stegmaier*	$450,333	4,333	$45	29	03/14
Two Rooms and a Boom *Alan Gerding and Sean McCoy*	$102,102	3,863	$20	31	10/13
The Undress *Dennis Caco*	$615,663	7,297	69	39	09/14

Project Name/Creator Name	Funding Total	Backer Total	Core Reward Price	Project Length (days)	Launch Date (mm/yy)
Viticulture *Jamey Stegmaier*	$65,980	942	$39	42	08/12
Where Art Thou, Romeo *Crash Games*	$5,723	2,188	$1	14	12/13
Xia: Legends of a Drift System *Cody Miller*	$346,772	3,293	$75	35	05/13

NOTES

Preface

1. Jamey Stegmaier, "Kickstarter Lessons," Kickstarter Lessons, http://www.kickstarterlessons.com.

Introduction

1. You can find the Kickstarter Lessons blog at www.kickstarterlessons.com. My personal blog is at www.jameystegmaier.com.

Chapter 1. You Don't Need to Launch Today

1. My Kickstarter Lessons blog is at www.kickstarterlessons.com; Funding the Dream is at www.buzzsprout.com/4646; and James Mathe's blog is at www.jamesmathe.com.

2. John Coveyou, "Kickstarter Stats 101: Does Backing Other Projects Matter?," Genius Games, October 25, 2014, http://gotgeniusgames.com/kickstarter-stats-101-backing-projects-matter.

Chapter 2. The Crowd Is the New Gatekeeper

1. Pebble Technology, Pebble: E-Paper Watch for iPhone and Android, https://www.kickstarter.com/projects/597507018/pebble-e-paper-watch-for-iphone-and-android.

2. *Ready Player One* was published by Random House in 2011.

3. The Secret Cabal Gaming Podcast, http://www.thesecretcabal.com/.

4. Simon Sinek, "How Great Leaders Inspire Action," TED, accessed February 15, 2015, http://www.ted.com/talks/simon_sinek_how_great_leaders_inspire_action.

Chapter 3. Crowdfunding Is the Rock Concert for Entrepreneurs

1. Blank Slate Press's Facebook page is http://www.facebook.com/pages/Blank-Slate-Press/288019896171; the e-newsletter sign-up page is at http://visitor.r20.constantcontact.com/manage/optin/ea?v=001k6dau0Gb9W8rDIC-PkypiA%3D%3D.

2. John Wrot, The King's Armory Board Game Campaign, https://www.indiegogo.com/projects/the-king-s-armory-board-game-campaign.

3. Alan Gerding, Boom or Doom! Kickstarter Adventures in the Tabletop World, https://www.kickstarter.com/projects/gerdling/boom-or-doom-kickstarter-adventures-in-the-tableto.

4. Alan Gerding and Sean McCoy, "Two Kickstarters and a Boom: Interview with the Creators," Stonemaier Games, November 6, 2013, http://stonemaiergames.com/two-kickstarters-and-a-boom-interview-with-a-creator.

5. Alan Gerding, Two Rooms and a Boom!, https://www.kickstarter.com/projects/gerdling/two-rooms-and-a-boom.

6. Michael Iachini, "How to Run a Humble Kickstarter Campaign," Clay Crucible Games, February 27, 2014, http://claycrucible.com/2014/02/how-to-run-a-humble-kickstarter-campaign.

7. Michael Mindes, Dungeon Roll—A Dicey Dungeon Delve, https://www.kickstarter.com/projects/michaelmindes/dungeon-roll-a-dicey-dungeon-delve.

8. Cesar Kuriyama, 1 Second Everyday App, https://www.kickstarter.com/projects/cesarkuriyama/1-second-everyday-app.

9. Michael Mindes, Coin Age—A Pay-What-You-Want Area Control Microgame, https://www.kickstarter.com/projects/michaelmindes/coin-age-a-pay-what-you-want-area-control-microgam.

10. Crash Games, Where Art Thou, Romeo?, https://www.kickstarter.com/projects/crashgames/where-art-thou-romeo.

11. Patrick Nickell, "A Peek Behind the Curtain of a True 'Pay What You Want' Kickstarter Campaign," Crash Games, February 12, 2014, http://crashgamesaz.com/a-peek-behind-the-curtain-of-a-true-pay-what-you-want-kickstarter-campaign.

Chapter 4. I Made These Mistakes So You Don't Have To

1. Luke Brown, The Beer Hammer, https://www.kickstarter.com/projects/1172715772/the-beer-hammer.

2. Wild Lens Inc., Bluebird Man, https://www.kickstarter.com/projects/157422504/bluebird-man.

Chapter 5. Make It about Them

1. Jason Zimdars, "Another 9999px," Signal vs. Noise, March 2, 2012, https://signalvnoise.com/posts/3126-another-9999px.

Chapter 6. Backers Are Individuals, Not Numbers

1. John Coveyou, "Kickstarter Stats 101: Should I Have a $1 Reward Level?" Genius Games, October 22, 2014, http://gotgeniusgames .com/kickstarter-stats-101-1-reward-level.
2. Daniel Pink, *To Sell Is Human* (New York: Riverhead Books, 2012), 158.
3. Ibid., 157–58.

Chapter 7. How to Make Friends and Lose Money

1. Simon Sinek, "Why Good Leaders Make You Feel Safe," TED, accessed February 15, 2015, http://www.ted.com/talks/simon_sinek_ why_good_leaders_make_you_feel_safe.
2. Jamey Stegmaier, "Shipping and Fulfillment," Stonemaier Games, accessed February 15, 2015, http://stonemaiergames.com/shipping-and-fulfillment.
3. CNNMoney, "Why 84% of Kickstarter's top projects shipped late," accessed February 15, 2015, http://money.cnn.com/interactive/ technology/kickstarter-projects-shipping.
4. Far Off Games, Xia: Legends of a Drift System, https://www.kick-starter.com/projects/1438045410/xia-legends-of-a-drift-system-0.

Chapter 8. Go Small to Win Big

1. "Nothing Succeeds Like Success," *The Economist*, March 3, 2014, http://www.economist.com/news/science-and-technology/21601494-and-science-has-now-proved-it-nothing-succeeds-success.
2. Pink, *To Sell Is Human*, 210–12.
3. Seth Godin, *The Icarus Deception: Why Make Art?*, https://www .kickstarter.com/projects/297519465/the-icarus-deception-why-make-art-new-from-seth-go.
4. Seth Godin, "Reflections on Today's Kickstarter," Seth Godin blog, June 18, 2012, http://sethgodin.typepad.com/seths_blog/2012/06/ reflections-on-todays-kickstarter.html.
5. Michael Domeny, "Hey You Guys"—Increasing Your Personal Connection with Backers," June 13, 2014, *League of Gamemakers*, http://www.leagueofgamemakers.com/hey-you-guys-increasing-your-personal-connection-with-backers/.

Chapter 9. Build a Better Community

1. SunTzuGames, Burning Suns, https://www.kickstarter.com/projects/suntzugames/burning-suns.
2. Aerjen Tamminga, Pleasant Dreams: A Card Game of Nightmares, https://www.kickstarter.com/projects/1143256637/pleasant-dreams-a-card-game-of-nightmares.
3. Natalya Alyssa Faden, Torn Armor, https://www.kickstarter.com/projects/alyssafaden/torn-armor.
4. Richard Bliss with Alyssa Faden, "Funding the Dream on Kickstarter Ep 134 Alyssa Faden Torn Armor," March 27, 2013, Funding the Dream, http://www.buzzsprout.com/4646/83899-funding-the-dream-on-kickstarter-ep-134-alyssa-faden-torn-armor.
5. David Montgomery and Marcelo Vital, Secret Around-the-World Adventures of Owney the Postal Dog, https://www.kickstarter.com/projects/194704400/secret-around-the-world-adventures-of-owney-the-po?ref=live.
6. Nikhil Arora and Alejandro Velez, TEDxPresidio, uploaded April 7, 2011, http://youtu.be/nboaE3O8zE8.
7. Nikhil Arora and Alejandro Velez, Home Aquaponics Kit: Self-Cleaning Fish Tank That Grows Food, https://www.kickstarter.com/projects/2142509221/home-aquaponics-kit-self-cleaning-fish-tank-that-g.

Chapter 10. Don't Quit Your Day Job ... Until You Quit Your Day Job

1. Erik Chevalier, "Terminus," The Doom That Came to Atlantic City, July 23, 2013, https://www.kickstarter.com/projects/forkingpath/the-doom-that-came-to-atlantic-city/posts/548030.

125 Crowdfunding Lessons in 125 Sentences

1. http://www.stonemaiergames.com/ks-lessons-full-list-chronological.

INDEX

ABOUT THE AUTHOR

Jamey Stegmaier is the cofounder and president of Stonemaier Games, publisher of Viticulture, Euphoria, Tuscany, Between Two Cities, Scythe, and several Treasure Chests of realistic components. He writes a crowdfunding blog along with a personal blog and the occasional work of fiction.  Jamey is an avid gamer, a voracious reader, a lover of movies, and a lifelong soccer player. Having graduated from Washington University in St. Louis in 2003, he now lives in St. Louis with his two cats, Biddy and Walter.

You can find Jamey on Twitter at @jameystegmaier or @stonemaiergames, on the Stonemaier Games Facebook page, or on any of these three websites:

www.kickstarterlessons.com
www.stonemaiergames.com
www.jameystegmaier.com.

Berrett–Koehler
Publishers

Berrett-Koehler is an independent publisher dedicated to an ambitious mission: *connecting people and ideas to create a world that works for all.*

We believe that to truly create a better world, action is needed at all levels—individual, organizational, and societal. At the individual level, our publications help people align their lives with their values and with their aspirations for a better world. At the organizational level, our publications promote progressive leadership and management practices, socially responsible approaches to business, and humane and effective organizations. At the societal level, our publications advance social and economic justice, shared prosperity, sustainability, and new solutions to national and global issues.

A major theme of our publications is "Opening Up New Space." Berrett-Koehler titles challenge conventional thinking, introduce new ideas, and foster positive change. Their common quest is changing the underlying beliefs, mindsets, institutions, and structures that keep generating the same cycles of problems, no matter who our leaders are or what improvement programs we adopt.

We strive to practice what we preach—to operate our publishing company in line with the ideas in our books. At the core of our approach is stewardship, which we define as a deep sense of responsibility to administer the company for the benefit of all of our "stakeholder" groups: authors, customers, employees, investors, service providers, and the communities and environment around us.

We are grateful to the thousands of readers, authors, and other friends of the company who consider themselves to be part of the "BK Community." We hope that you, too, will join us in our mission.

A BK Business Book

This book is part of our BK Business series. BK Business titles pioneer new and progressive leadership and management practices in all types of public, private, and nonprofit organizations. They promote socially responsible approaches to business, innovative organizational change methods, and more humane and effective organizations.

Berrett–Koehler
Publishers

Connecting people and ideas
to create a world that works for all

Dear Reader,

Thank you for picking up this book and joining our worldwide community of Berrett-Koehler readers. We share ideas that bring positive change into people's lives, organizations, and society.

To welcome you, we'd like to offer you a free e-book. You can pick from among twelve of our bestselling books by entering the promotional code BKP92E here: http://www.bkconnection.com/welcome.

When you claim your free e-book, we'll also send you a copy of our e-newsletter, the *BK Communiqué*. Although you're free to unsubscribe, there are many benefits to sticking around. In every issue of our newsletter you'll find

- A free e-book
- Tips from famous authors
- Discounts on spotlight titles
- Hilarious insider publishing news
- A chance to win a prize for answering a riddle

Best of all, our readers tell us, "Your newsletter is the only one I actually read." So claim your gift today, and please stay in touch!

Sincerely,

Charlotte Ashlock
Steward of the BK Website

Questions? Comments? Contact me at bkcommunity@bkpub.com.

MIX
From responsible
sources
FSC® C113845

Certified
Corporation
bcorporation.net